Write That Script! and Write it Now!

L. J. Sedgwick

An introduction to screenwriting

This edition | 2018

D1437845

Janey Mac Books

Formatting by Polgarus Studio
Cover Design by www.designbos.ie

Print Version
ISBN-13: 978-0995702745 (Janey Mac Books)
ISBN-10: 0995702748

Published by Janey Mac Books 2018

Contents

1: Visual Storytelling: An Introduction

20 years from now, you will be more disappointed by the things you didn't do than by the things you did... Sail away from the safe harbour. Explore. Dream.

- Mark Twain

The best advice I ever got was when I was 16 and wanted to write scripts. "You can't write your second script until you've written your first."

That's what this book is for. To enable you to get your first script down, on the screen or the page, without overcomplicating the process. It's full of tips, exercises, advice and just enough theory to inspire you to write that first draft.

Now.

Not next year or sometime in the future when you have more time, fewer obligations or commitments.

Now.

Before we start, list the first five films you remember seeing.

What do you remember about them? Was it something to do with the story or characters, with the location or atmosphere?

Hold on to this, we'll come back to it later.

Now list five films you wish you had written. Again, why?

Take a few minutes more to list five memorable screen moments, five characters you have never forgotten, five images you remember vividly.

From all of this, what is your definition of a great film?

For me, a great film is one that people are still talking about afterwards. As a writer, that's what you need to achieve with your screenplay. You want readers to remember your characters, your story and your writing.

That they love the characters or hate them; either is good so long as they want to meet with you to discuss how they can bring your screenplay to life.

Do you have what it takes?

Screenwriting is a concise medium. It's tight. It's visual.

When compared to other mediums, it is demanding. Everything on the page has to have a reason to be there, because time is short. For the same reason, there are rules and limitations imposed by the medium. This book is about learning to use (or subvert) them to write a stronger script.

And it is worth it. I've written in many mediums but what never grows old about screenwriting is the buzz that comes when a character steps off the page, when a sequence of scenes works, when a small detail or something a character does now tells the story in a way it might have taken me five scenes to do when I started writing for the screen.

To be a screenwriter you need imagination, a yearning or hunger to write, stamina and craft. Craft you can learn; the rest are your own. With practice, you can make them work harder for you in pursuit of your final script.

You wouldn't have picked up this book if you didn't have the imagination to dream up an idea. Now you have to envisage it as a finished script. The daily grind of normal working life often forces imagination to a low frequency. The exercises in this book are designed to turn the volume up. Writing a strong and original script requires imagining scenes, locations, characters, drama, conflict, even how the sky and ground will look on occasion so that you avoid cliché.

But the *yearning* is what has brought you to this book. It will get you beyond writer's block and help you meet deadlines. Because of it, you will even turn down interesting social occasions in order to write. Feed this yearning by writing what excites you. Then it will get you to the end of the script and beyond.

By the middle of this book, you will know what you need to do in order to finish your script. That's where stamina comes in, pushing you through to the end, regardless.

On then to craft

Knowing the craft of screenwriting will help you to avoid rolling up to page seventy-five in a hundred-page script only to realise you don't know where you're going, or that you have become bored with the story because there isn't enough depth to it.

Alternatively, nobody wants to use the craft purely to write a competent, formulaic script, exactly ninety minutes long that offers nothing new, that lacks an original voice and energy.

Whatever you have in your head now, that's where you begin. It could be an idea, a character or a theme, a snippet from the newspaper or the germ of a world you want to explore. Several of my projects began with character, some with story, one with a situation. Another started with a location that intrigued me, while others grew from an issue, theme or anecdote that I wanted to explore.

I've tried to provide examples for every point I make so that it's easy to see them work in a practical sense. Some are of my own invention and others are from well known films. I've used a wide selection of films because that's the way to see that the points I make apply over a wide and varied range of films. There's a list of the films I cite and their writers in **Appendix D**.

As for the exercises, they are tried and tested with screenwriting students at all levels over many years. They will help you to open up your story, even encourage you to take a few risks with it, to develop your idea and your characters in depth. Some are designed to kick-start your muse into misbehaving creatively so that your idea will be as original and unique as you can make it. Others are more practical, designed to enable you to put the theory into practice and to help you finish your first draft.

While some of the exercises might challenge you a bit; others will come quite naturally. Doing them will make you a stronger writer.

There is no one 'right way' to start a screenplay. What I have tried to do in this book is gather together the tools you will need. The rest is up to you. Your goal is to finish your first full screenplay. It won't be perfect – it's a first draft – but it's the only way to learn and you will feel fantastic when you finish.

Hold onto that because, at times, it will feel like a rocky road!

TIP: Always keep scraps of paper handy. (A proper notebook can be too intimidating at the start.) If you get an idea for a snatch of a scene, an exchange of dialogue, some characteristic behaviour or an image, write it down.

Such ideas may never come again. Some of the heart of your story may be on those pages. One of these snatches can be enough to re-energise your story after you've plotted your narrative or when you're feeling weighed down by it. Or it may be your very next screenplay!

Exercise:

The opening image

Let's get your visual imagination acting before we get into the gritty stuff. More than any other medium, in screenwriting everything counts, whether it's a dust cloud, a shootout or a centipede running over a polished boot.

Conventional wisdom is that an audience decides within ten minutes whether it will invest emotionally in a film. With the advent of Netflix, I suspect that time may be shrinking because at home there are no social constraints (such as pushing past other audience members to leave the cinema) while the zapper is so close!

Understanding this, let's think of the opening image in a script. It has to intrigue us and make us turn the page.

The poppy field

You have a poppy field. Think of ten different ways of seeing this field and what it might look like. If it's flowering, if it's lush, if it's diseased, if it's an opium farm, if it's in a warehouse, on a spaceship, if it's small or vast, if the sun is shining or not, if it's being projected onto a wall.

1. Now, what can you hear?

What five sounds might you connect with a poppy field? Insects, birds, animals, the weather, voices – are there any? Do the noises match what we see? Are they a recording played on a old-fashioned tape-deck, a CD or live?

Now think of five sounds you wouldn't associate with a poppy field. These might be off-screen or on, beneath the ground or in the air.

2. Playing with genre

Okay, now how would you describe this poppy field if you were using it as the opening image/ location in a range of different genres? Try this with three or more of the following:

- Sci-fi,
- Rom-com,
- Drama,
- Historical,
- Soap,
- Horror,
- Kids,
- Comedy,
- Something else entirely.

While deciding on what to show us, also consider what you want us to feel: comfortable, nervous, curious, scared?

3. Now add action

What happens after this opening image?

It's up to you – but don't limit yourself. Push it as far as you can go and then twist it again. Be as absurd or ridiculous or weird as you like. Surreal, if that works.

If you are writing horror, thriller or sci-fi, maybe you opened with a sunny, warm scene and now you disturb your audience with some image/ sound/ lack of sound/ the behaviour of a character already in the scene or arriving.

The point is that you are in control of your reader's emotions as they read your script and see it unfold in their heads. You know how you want them to feel. Think up a number of options and pick one that's interesting, different, that you haven't seen before. Maybe a child's scream cuts across the peaceful or beautiful visuals, or we hear laughter off screen. Maybe we see a pair of forbidden lovers being hunted down or picnicking, hear music or sounds that jar with what we are seeing. Do we hear disembodied instructions or no sound at all?

~ ~ ~

It should be clear to you now that nobody thinks visually in the same way as you do. No two people doing this exercise will come up with the same collection of images or sounds.

As a writer, you draw on all your memories – consciously and subconsciously, on your experiences and your perspective. Everything you need to write a wholly original script is within you, but sometimes you have to be willing to push it a little.

Brainstorming like this is a way of stoking a reluctant or recumbent imagination to come up with alternative, even disjointed images, sounds, visuals, any one of which could make your opening image or scene utterly unique and compelling.

2: Your Idea: What You Need For a Screenplay

"If it can be written or thought, then it can be filmed."

— Stanley Kubrick

Many scripts are written but few are chosen for development. Fewer still go on into production – so yours has to stand out. This is where story comes in.

An idea is buzzing in your head – or maybe just nudging you in the ribs at regular intervals. It would be great on the screen, small or large. How do you make sure this idea has the ingredients you need for it to work as a screenplay?

1. You need strong, credible, sympathetic characters

My experience reading, writing and pitching scripts is that if the characters are strong and compelling this can be enough to incite a face-to-face meeting with a producer who is interested in your writing. Even if that particular script isn't chosen for further development by the people you are talking to, it should lead to an open invitation to talk about other ideas.

2. You need to find a story you are passionate about and willing to live with for two years

The best work is often driven by obsession. Ideally you feel this is a story only you can write. Now answer these three questions:

- Why do you need to tell this story?
- Why now?
- What's your particular angle?

The next challenge is to find a way of communicating your story visually so it excites others in the same way. You are going to translate something that you dreamt up into a written and visual medium that will have an impact on other people's minds! This is the magical element that will keep you writing (and rewriting, but more of that later).

Regarding the old adage of 'write what you know', I would add, *write what interests you to know*. Don't be intimidated by what don't know. Human nature will drive your story; everything else can be researched or learnt.

However, if it requires research, only write that story if the research interests you, because it can be time-consuming and make sure you discipline yourself to stop researching and write when the time is right.

Now what does this story need to work as a screenplay?

Dramatic narrative

It may sound obvious, but your story must have a dramatic narrative that will keep us turning the pages and, ultimately, watching the screen. The first part of this is that your central character needs a goal. There is something she wants more than anything else. It's worth noting that she may not realise how badly she wants it at the start of your script, or may even be in pursuit of some other (lesser) goal.

Once she has a goal, you have the dramatic question that will frame your screenplay: *Will she succeed or fail?*

To make this question interesting, you need to make it difficult for your central character to succeed. Conflict will come from obstacles you create and can place in her path to make it extremely and increasingly difficult for her to succeed in reaching her goal.

Obstacles should come in all sorts of forms – mental, psychological, physical. Their purpose is to keep your central character on her toes and your readers on the edge of their seats.

Not only does this conflict have to keep coming but you create tension by ensuring that the stakes keep rising, no matter what action she takes.

What do we mean by stakes?

Stakes are anything that is important to your central character, the price she risks paying by continuing to pursue her goal. Initially, it may be losing access to information, losing her car, her income or her reputation. Later on it may be losing her life, her lover, her family, her identity, her sanity, her life or the lives of those she loves or the destruction of her community.

As readers, we become concerned for her as she struggles to overcome more and more difficult obstacles. We should want her to succeed, *against the odds*. When she succeeds or fails, you have answered the dramatic question you set-up at the start and the film is all but done.

Without this conflict, we won't get emotionally engaged; the story will go flat or drift.

Now let's move on to the essence of the story you want to write. I'll return to conflict later.

Going in deep: your special angle

Themes are large and intellectual. Ideally, your story has a theme that is universal and to which we can all relate. But you must believe in it too, at a deeper level. It can be useful to find out where your interest in this theme stems from so that you can tap into the raw emotion that is driving you to investigate a story like this.

Let's say your story is about injustice. We all understand injustice at an intellectual level, but many scripts are about injustice. What will make your story different is what lies beneath this generic theme. What specific injustice are you exploring? Maybe it's about:

- spending half your life in jail for something you didn't do.
- being the sibling who isn't favoured by her parents.
- being passed over, time and again, for promotion.

Now let's move closer to the core, nearer to something to which we can all relate on a personal or experiential level: What is your story really about, for your main character?

- Discovering her best friend has lied to her all her life?
- Never being good enough for her parents?
- Being unable to stand up for herself?

Now go one stage deeper: What is it about for you? What's the core emotion driving your interest in this theme? Could it be:

- The need to know the truth, whatever the cost?
- The fear of being left alone?
- The need to be heard?
- The need to succeed at any cost?

If theme is intellectual – an idea or an issue – what you are looking for now is the emotional, personal, *visceral* reason you want to write this particular story. It may come from your first awareness of an emotion, of feeling personally connected to this issue or it may come from life experience.

For example, you may be writing a story about a public injustice or a thriller about a prison breakout but, deep down, what is driving you to write this story in *this particular way* is your experience of loss or fear or helplessness. Whatever emotion you discover driving your story will be one that you have personal and visceral experience of and bringing that to the table will make your story stronger. It means you are writing this story in a way that is unique to you.

Discovering the emotional truth that makes you want to write this story will allow you to access a rich vein of possible images, characters, situations that nobody else has. You can raid your own imagination and memories. It can also give you a greater drive to finish.

Your readers may never be aware of this emotional truth but it will help you to write your story, to know what scenes to include and what ones don't fit as well as what flaws and strengths to give characters and where you need the story to go.

It may also help you to choose:

- Between different options and different obstacles.
- When to start the story and when to end.
- Secondary characters and subplots that will help you to explore your theme.

Once you know where your story comes from, you can look for conflict to roll into the path of your central character.

Creating conflict

You can extract obstacles from a number of sources:

1. Internal

Internal conflict comes from your central character's flaws, weaknesses, unresolved issues or attitudes. Even perceived strengths might work against her achieving her goal. If she sees herself as never ever needing help, for example, then her inability to ask for or accept help at a critical point will most likely lead to further difficulties. If she's afraid of the colour red, surely she is bound to need to enter a red room to get an essential clue at some stage?

As with the stakes, the flaws you choose will depend on your story and your genre. This is by far the most interesting source of drama in most screenplays.

> TIP: Don't forget to consider that the way your protagonist interprets outside events because of her past could also cause conflict.

2. External (people)

Here, you're looking at your cast. These are the people with whom you choose to surround your central character. They all have opinions, attitudes and goals. To make life interesting for your central character, which of these could be working against or with her, for or against her goal? Consider workplace issues, home life issues, relationships.

To create drama, your central character needs an antagonist, whether she goes up against an individual or an organisation (such as the Church, Mafia, the media industry). Regardless of whether they are on screen or out of sight for much of the screenplay, it is very useful to give the reader someone tangible to hate or fear.

Of course, conflict that comes from your supporting cast may not be seen by them as opposition. Your central character's life partner, for example, could be working against her achieving her goal 'for her own good'. Maybe one character simply has a trait that hinders your central character's progress at some critical point. Let's say her best friend has an uncontrollable temper. What if, because of it, your central character loses access to a witness, to a piece of information, to her child?

> TIP: Don't lose sight of the fact that every member of your cast has an opinion on most of the rest of your cast and especially your protagonist. You can use this to create additional opposition or difficulties for your central character and her quest.

3. External (environment)

This could be anything in the environment through which your story moves. It could be a torrential downpour, a tyre bursting on her car, a pothole in the road, an elevator that breaks down; anything that causes problems for your central character.

4. Extra-/ super-natural

This is the universe making life difficult, or another dimension entirely. It's beyond her control. It could be seen as bad luck but you are the one who decides if it contributes to your story.

~ ~ ~

As you can see, obstacles can be anything and not merely events or actions by characters in your script. If you feel stuck, ask yourself, what's the worst thing that could happen to my character now? Or what's the best? – so that you can make it backfire later.

The challenge

By its very nature, the demands of a feature film impose constrictions on a story. Once you know what they are and why they exist, you can use them to tell your story more powerfully and effectively.

Character

Most films run around ninety minutes in length. This is roughly ninety to one hundred properly formatted pages. (See **Appendix A**) Characters are our way into the story but you only have time within a feature script to develop between four and six credible three-dimensional characters. If there are too many characters for us to follow, they may feel like ciphers because you haven't time to give them depth. In this case, they can stop helping your story.

Time span

Screenwriting is compressed storytelling. There is no time to waste. Everything has to count; every gesture, every flowerpot, every scene. If you doubt this, think how long a bad film feels, while you don't even realise time has passed during a good one.

Story

Because your central character will (traditionally) be redeemed by the end of your script, **backstory** is critical if we are to understand her motivation. **Exposition** is the revelation of the information we need to know for the story to work.

But screenwriting is a visual medium and your audience is canny, so how you reveal necessary information can be tricky. Telling an audience *anything*, especially if they don't yet need to know, is not allowed! It happens all the time but you can do better. It's up to you as the writer to find a way for readers to discover this information without feeling they have been preached at or spoon-fed.

Your own attention span

Writing a feature film is a long-term project. Are you prepared to commit? To rewrite, at a future date? Possibly several times? To have and to hold long after a sane and sensible person (probably not a writer!) would have given up?

Exercises

1. Why this story?

Every writer explores certain themes over and over in their creative work. A feature film with a theme about overcoming failure might have an underlying theme, for the writer, of loss. While these themes may not seem obvious to anyone reading or watching your work, knowing what yours are can help you to enrich the screenplay and story in a subtle and imaginative way.

Make a list of themes and issues that fascinate you. Can you trace any of them back to where that issue first became important to you or when you became aware of them, as if you were a character in your own script?

2. Look and learn

Consider five films you've recently watched, or five episodes of a series. See if you can identify both theme and emotional heart.

3: Creating Character: Beyond Cliché

"Don't expect the puppets of your mind to become the people of your story. If they are not realities in your own mind, there is no mysterious alchemy in ink and paper that will turn wooden figures into flesh and blood."

– Leslie Gordon Barnard

Characters are what make a film memorable. I would argue that for every film you remember vividly, there will be a character or characters that stand out. Think of the vultures in *The Jungle Book*, the little boy, Samuel (Lukas Haas) in *Witness*, Princess Leia (Carrie Fisher) or Han Solo (Harrison Ford) in *Star Wars*.

Think back to the answers you gave to those questions about films in Chapter 1. I would guess that character is at the root of why you remember most, if not all of them. For me, everything flows from character. It's their journey we follow; their stories, their conflict that keeps us perched on the edge of our seats.

But unless we believe in them, we're not going to be anxious about their safety or the mistakes they make. This is often where first drafts, even perfectly structured ones, fall down. How your story progresses, what it shapes into and, to a large extent, how gripping it will be relies on the characters with which you populate it. They can also be the most exciting thing about writing scripts. You are, literally, bringing people to life.

What's the point of creating a one-dimensional character?

Even a two-dimensional one?

Make them real. Interesting. Fun.

Memorable for the right reasons!

Generally, once you have the right characters, you cannot imagine telling the story through others. This is why it's worth putting the work in to create characters with enough complexity to carry your story, whatever their role in it.

This is your responsibility as a writer. Every character you breathe life into must feel real, even if they only exist for one crucial moment in your screenplay. For this to happen, they have to have genuine depth.

One little cautionary note! In my experience, the 'bad guys' can be easier to conceive, especially in scripts that started out as tight, high concept stories. While these stories were generally the easiest films to pitch, they were often the most difficult to write the central characters for. I think this is because twisted, damaged, dangerous characters can simply be far more fun to write. The danger is that your central character feels a bit weak and insipid in comparison. Since our central characters are the people we want our readers to be rooting for, the challenge then is to create central characters who can match these antagonists (and their allies) in terms of charisma, courage, inventiveness or pure humanity.

Unearthing Character...

Essentially, you unearth character by exploring their lives in two parts:

- Their past or biography: what has happened to them in their lives up to the point when your story begins
- The 'here and now': who they are at this point in time

Benefits of exploring character in this way

- You will unearth a character's set of inbuilt reactions, attitudes and patterns of behaviour.

Let's say you decide your central character works for a charity organisation and that she was abandoned as a child. How she is *now*, as a result of what happened *then*, will inform her behaviour and the choices she makes in your screenplay. So you may decide that her backstory has made her tough on those who let adversity grind them down. Or that she is drawn to those who are ruthless about their own survival.

Alternatively, her background may have made her (dangerously?) empathetic.

Each of those choices allow you to create an entirely different character and each of these characters will make different choices when faced with the same situation.

- Less rewriting.

On a practical level, doing this work now means that there should be less rewriting down the line. You will know what makes your characters tick before you begin; how they will react in any given scene under certain conditions. This does not mean your characters won't still keep surprising you as you write your script, but they should do so in a credible way that is consistent with character and with motivation.

You will soon know if something doesn't fit.

You will also know what needs to happen for you to make life difficult for your central character, what is important to her, how to create the world she lives in and how to blow it apart.

The risk of not investing time in some character development work is that you could end up with a screenplay that operates well on the level of plot and structure but lacks character depth and credibility.

For supporting characters, less work is required but it can be worth doing some of this.

- Shades of grey ensure that they feel real and not like cardboard cut-outs.
- It can also suggest connections and threads between characters that can be interesting or useful.

Biography

A character's **biography** is defined as anything of relevance that has happened before the moment your story begins. You are looking for the process or events that have formed the character. They are not necessarily major events or experiences but they will influence her behaviour, attitudes, issues and point of view (POV).

Biography reveals character. The answers you come up with will suggest locations, secondary characters, even crucial plot points/scenes/events/motivations for other characters you would never have considered before.

Those parts of her biography that you will use to inform her behaviour within your story are her **backstory**. These are the moments or events in her past that explain her motivation, emotional need, her strengths and her weaknesses.

So what questions should you ask?

Questions # 1: Childhood

What was your character's childhood like? What were her early relationships like with family, friends or locals? What does she remember from this time and how does she remember it? Are there aspects of it that she has locked away at the back of her mind or parts that she celebrates and credits with shaping the person she has become?

Why go so far back? Because someone born in the middle of a large family will have had a different set of experiences than that of an only child, or of a child who has been orphaned, adopted, bullied, was homeless, lived on the street with her parent(s) and so on.

A person who has grown up in a wide-open space may find city living challenging or wonderful for different reasons. These reasons might be illustrated by the way she lives, how she dresses, decorates her living space, walks, talks, sleeps and how comfortable she is with other people. Those differences could be the key to her motivation within your story.

- Where did she grow up? (On a farm, in a tiny apartment, with alcoholic parents, with grandparents, in another country, under another name, etc?)
- What sort of childhood did she have? (Happy, sad, neglected, oppressed…?)
- Did anything change dramatically during her childhood/adolescence?

Biography can also indicate useful and interesting overlaps between characters. For example, two characters deeply dislike each other. What if you decide there are similarities in their backgrounds? How could you use those similarities to affect how their relationship develops within your story?

Questions # 2: Relationships

- What is your character's relationship history?
- How does she feel about her siblings? Her parents?
- Does she have friends from her past? If so, how strong are these friendships? How have they altered with time?
- Does she find it hard or easy to make friends and if so, does she know why?

The level to which you go depends on a character's importance within the story. Perhaps two characters share a passion for old black-and-white thrillers. Could you use this detail to help you tell your story? Maybe an argument between them happens in a theatre showing such a film or *The Maltese Falcon* (written by John Huston, based on the Dashiell Hammett novel) might be playing at an open-air cinema and they choose to pretend they haven't seen each other rather than spoil the film. Might one of them quote from a certain film when under stress? Could one of them chop up the old DVD of a film that the other treasures in spite, or steal it?

Questions # 3: Memories and mind

Now, since this is your story, ask your character questions that feel important to you. Try not to limit yourself to questions that seem immediately relevant to your story. Go off tangent and see what you can find. Draw on your own experiences, memories and imagination to fill out their pasts. For example:

- What are her earliest memories, best and worst?
- What are her hopes, wishes, fears?
- Where do these come from?
- When did she first become aware of them?

Basically, having interrogated your characters, you are now mining their past for possible backstory elements that will explain who these people are.

The 'here and now'

Now you want to see your characters as they are, warts and all; as they perceive themselves to be, how aware they are of their past, what motivates them and so on.

Questions you could ask might include:

- What is her goal in life? Does she have more than one?
- How far will she go to satisfy this need and in what way?
- What does she need, emotionally? Does she know?
- How has she tried to satisfy this need?
- How does she feel about herself? About her life? Her job? Her current relationships?

Depending on your story, theme and emotional centre of your story, you may ask different questions:

- If she had to be a superhero, who would she be? Why?
- What animation character does she most identify with? Why?
- What food will she never ever eat? Why?

- What's her favourite TV programme?
- What did she dream of last?

Bringing it all together

How do you use all this information to create a three-dimensional character? For a start, you want to know how she views the world. This is her point of view (POV) and since it's formed before your story begins, it will flavour her behaviour, attitude and personality. What you need to know now, however, is how she *behaves* as a result, both in company and when alone.

For example, if a character believes herself to be ethical, is she a human rights activist, does she boycott products from unethical companies, or merely talk about human rights and equality but do nothing?

How will each of these behaviours affect your story?

What difficulties could her behaviour throw up in terms of the central storyline and character relationships?

You also want to know how she *feels*, both towards herself and towards others. What you are looking for now are attitudes, of which she may be unaware or in denial, that could make it difficult for her to achieve her goal, whatever her role in the story. (See **Attitude**, Chapter 12.)

For example, you may decide that a character's need is 'to be heard' but that she feels superior to those with whom she is dealing. As a result, she keeps antagonising the very people she needs to listen to her.

What type of personality does your character have?

Is she pessimistic or optimistic, witty or dry, impulsive or pedantic? Once you decide, you can look for traits through which you can reveal her personality to us.

The choices are boundless.

If she is optimistic, does she always respond with an '*At least...*' to any negative comment? Does she refuse to give up when it's obvious that something won't work? Does she get caught out in the rain because she refuses to believe the weather will change? Is the optimism a front for someone who is genuinely depressed or a way of keeping truth at bay? Of keeping a distance from the people around her or because she's surrounded by pessimists and knows her optimistic attitude annoys them? Does she refuse to listen to 'negative' advisors only to buy a sofa that won't fit in her flat unless it's on its side?

If your character is angry – how does she react? By throwing something, kicking a passing animal, holding all the anger in (until later, perhaps) or roaring fake swear words? If she is trying to hide an emotion, how would she do this? Is she always late at work because she dreads the boredom, is wary of her boss, afraid to leave her child alone with her mother or because she can't organise her life right now?

The point I'm making is that it is only by seeing how your characters behave in the dramatic circumstances you create that your readers and eventual viewers get to know your characters.

As for backstory

What you choose to reveal of a character's past will help us understand her motivation, to empathise or sympathise with her.

But, and it's a big warningful '*but*':

Not everything you create as your character's backstory needs to be revealed.

Let's say there is some traumatic event in a character's past of which we need to be aware at a certain point in your screenplay. Might it be more powerful if she is unable to talk coherently about what happened, if she tries to tell us and has to stop than if she can tell us exactly what happened in the past?

Think of how much you need us to know and what you want us to feel as readers. Give us no more than that, and move on.

How and when you reveal *anything* about your character is critical. Readers should never be *told* that a character has a chip on her shoulder. It should become clear to us by how that character acts and reacts within the screenplay or how other people respond to her, in a way that feels natural or understandable.

For example, if she overreacts to something another character says about how hard they worked to get to where they are today or simply snorts in derision. Maybe another character makes some comment about it being less a chip than a redwood forest on her shoulders. (See also **Exposition** in Chapter 8 and **Flashbacks** in Chapter 15.)

Be creative and see where it leads

Don't worry, the theory becomes instinctive. You don't consciously say, "I'm not going to write a line of dialogue for this character until I know if she's left-handed". But, while developing her, you might think, *Would it be interesting if she was left-handed?*

And, more importantly, *Why?*

The answers you might find could include:

Because left-handed people are meant to be creative.

Because at the time she was schooled, children weren't allowed to be left-handed and this led to all sorts of issues, psychological and physical. Could it have left scars that impact upon her behaviour now and her attitude to authority figures, to the Religious, to young people who are allowed freedoms she never had, to a squishing of her artistic abilities, to a career she hates and so on?

See? It's fun!

What if she had to wear glasses from the age of seven? How could this have affected her? In the past: teasing, nicknames, bullying, missing out on things she couldn't see, self-consciousness. In the present: what if her glasses break, if she has had laser treatment, if she never wears her glasses on a first date, if she become a workaholic because she avoided relationships or an artist because she could finally see the detail of the world at age seven and it has been a wonder ever since?

Depth of character

What you are looking for when you develop a character are experiences or memories that have shaped her. The process will often reveal traits that wouldn't have been obvious to you when you started developing your story but you will have come up with more than you can use.

This is a good thing. It means you will now make choices from a position of strength.

Complexity of character comes from how your characters react and from the choices they make, but time is limited in a screenplay. How your characters behave will reveal them to us and one tiny detail can have reverberations that will help you tell your story.

So pick the traits that will be most helpful to your story and don't be worried about letting some of the detail you have unearthed sink into the background. Nothing is wasted. The material you don't use is under the surface making your character real.

Exercises

These are for those idle moments when a bus is late, when you have some time with nothing to do but check Facebook. Put your phone on aeroplane mode and challenge yourself to think of answers to a couple of questions about some of your characters.

Remember, there is no right or wrong answer. Something you put down initially for one character might transfer to a different character or change entirely as you get to know your characters better.

The point is that you don't need a lot of time or even a notebook to start putting your characters together. Use scraps of paper, bus tickets or the 'notes' app on your phone.

1. A BASIC QUESTIONNAIRE:

- Name?
- Nickname? If she has one, when did she get it and why?
- Gender?
- Place of birth?
- Age?
- Current occupation? Previous job?
- Does she enjoy her job? What hours does she work? Does she have friends at work? Is she ambitious? Is there something else she aspires to do?
- How does she feel about herself/ career/ her relationships?
- What did she dream of doing as a child?
- What is the most important person/ thing in her life
- Goal: What does she want more than anything? Does she know? How far is she willing to go to succeed? What is she willing to lose/ risk in order to succeed?
- What is her emotional need? Is she aware of it? Where does it come from?
- Strengths: what skills or talents does she have? Does she recognise, hide or deny them?
- Flaws: What is she most afraid of and why? What is she weak at and would she acknowledge it?
- If she could be anyone, who would she be? If she could be any animal, what would she choose to be?
- What does she do when she's alone? Does she have a hobby? Is it a secret? When did she start this hobby?
- Her appearance, how does she dress? Is it important? What does she wear when she's alone, when she goes to bed, if she's trying to make a good impression?
- How does she laugh? What makes her cry? What makes her nervous, sad, uncomfortable?
- Who does she admire or detest?
- Now add any questions of your own…

4: Playing Devil's Advocate: Creating Your Protagonist

"I think the deeper you go into questions, the deeper or more interesting the questions get. And I think that's the job of art."

— Andre Debus III

Finding the right protagonist for your story is crucial.

Think of *Amadeus*, written by Peter Shaffer. How different would that story have been if the narrator had been Mozart himself, his wife, a servant girl, a mistress, an historian or an unrecognised love-child looking back?

Imagine if *In The Name Of The Father* (written by Terry George and Jim Sheridan) had been told from the viewpoint of Paul Hill (John Lynch) rather than Gerry Conlon (Daniel Day-Lewis)? If Nurse Ratched had been written as the central character in the film version of Ken Kesey's *One Flew Over the Cuckoo's Nest* (screenplay by Laurence Hauben & Bo Goldman)? This is, after all, how she sees herself, with McMurphy (Jack Nicholson) as her antagonist.

What if Helen Hunt's character (Carol) in *As Good As It Gets* (written by Mark Andrus and James L. Brooks) was telling the story of Melvin Udall (Jack Nicholson)? If, in *Maudie* (written by Sherry White), Maudie's husband Everett (Ethan Hawke) was the central character rather than Maudie (Sally Hawkins) herself?

Think of five films you loved and three that disappointed. Take a moment to switch the characters around. If a different character, even one not in the actual film, had been the central character. Imagine the differences, possibilities and options available.

Your choice of central character affects where the story starts, what elements you include in the mix, what events you choose to show and how they run.

Everything.

It's a big decision.

Huge.

She is the main way for your readers to get into the script. You want us to connect with her and we will do so if we understand her motivation and what she is up against. At the very least, you need us to sympathise with her plight as this will pull us in but, ideally, we will empathise with her. In so doing, we *become* her.

Once you have chosen the right central character, you won't be able to imagine telling the story from any other point of view. So, even if you're certain you have the right lead for your screenplay, look at your story idea and ask yourself, *Is this the point of view that is the most interesting or challenging one for telling this story?* Have you considered other characters, changing the gender, the age of the central character or what relationships you include?

Who to choose?

How can you identify your central character?

- Your central character sets the story in motion, even if it is unwillingly or without intention. This story is her story.
- Her actions have the greatest influence on what happens.
- She has the most to win or lose. It may be life, sanity, family, love, health, career.
- Her objective is the story purpose. When she achieves or fails to reach her goal, the story is (mostly) told.
- We identify with her most strongly.
- Classic central characters tend to be active, energetic, attractive and flawed.
- Her value system is generally different from that of the world she inhabits. It often tends to mirror the writer's own and it shapes the story.
- Out of all your characters, she has the greatest potential for change.

What does she need?

To have potential for change, your central character has to have an emotional need that has not been met. Yet. She may be unaware or in denial of this need but it comes from her past. Whatever happened then changed her forever.

This doesn't necessarily mean it was a big or traumatic event or series of events. As I was once told, you can stand under a waterfall or a dripping tap, you still get wet. What matters is the impact whatever happened had on her. It left her 'flawed' in the context of your story.

As a result of what happened, she needs to be loved/ accepted/left alone/ famous/ rich/ feared/ heard/ seen; whatever is most useful for your narrative.

Her emotional need provides her with a stronger motivation than anyone else could have, creating the dramatic tension that will hold us in our seats. Even if you choose never to reveal what happened within the script, you do need to know this critical part of her backstory before you begin.

Once you know her need, you can find obstacles anywhere. The value of these obstacles will become clearer when we start plotting but essentially obstacles lead to conflict. Conflict in turn leads to drama, the lifeblood of the screenplay, whether it's an action movie, a thriller, a rom-com or a drama.

How does this work?

Let's say her emotional need is 'to be heard'. The complication you throw in her path to success could be physical: she gets laryngitis at the wrong time, a crucial moment in your script when she has to deliver a talk that will save her company, the planet, her life or the life of a loved one. It might simply be that you put her in an environment filled with deafening noise so that she can't even hear her own thoughts and misses some important clue.

The complications could also be emotional. For example, if she becomes speechless in the face of something awful happening to her or those she loves.

What are her strengths and weaknesses?

Your central character needs to be flawed. A vulnerable side makes her human, someone with whom it is easier to identify. This allows your readers to bond with her over the course of your screenplay as they learn more about her.

Strengths you might give her could be the ability to do complex maths in her head, extreme fitness, empathy, puzzle-solving, a belief in justice. Her weaknesses might be her inability to trust people, fear of flying, stubbornness.

If these seem random listed here, the point is that when you create your own central character you are looking for strengths and flaws that will help you to create conflict for her. Then, if you fancy, you can add little extras that will increase her audience appeal such as quick thinking, wittiness, charisma, sexiness or some unusual talent such as the ability to do magic tricks.

Of course, these can rebound against her too!

Essentially, you choose traits for your central character that will be useful to you. If you give her an ability to whistle, at some stage that has to be relevant to your story. It might even save her life by allowing her to indicate where she is when she is buried under rubble.

Often the final, most difficult block to her succeeding is recognising and either overcoming or acting despite her internal flaw or weakness.

How do you use these to make us care?

As your central character struggles and overcomes obstacles, we will discover more and more admirable strengths. We gain more and more reasons to have confidence in her, while still aware of the real possibility that she may fail.

This doubt adds excitement.

Active and energetic

I mentioned before that conventional central characters tend to be active and energetic. These are for pragmatic reasons, in terms of audience and story.

- As readers and viewers, most of us find these traits appealing and attractive.

- These characteristics ensure that your central character will often behave unpredictably. She will act without thinking, befriend or trust the wrong people, make impulsive decisions and so on. All of which leads to greater conflict and drama, driving the story forward.
- Such traits also allow the potential for surprise.

TIP: A strength can become a weakness and vice versa. For example, stubbornness makes it difficult for your central character to take advice from anyone. But it could become the tenacity she needs to refuse to give up, despite the odds, when anyone else would. In those circumstances, it becomes an admirable trait.

What does she value?

Values are what separate your central character from the world although she may not realise it at beginning. For example, in *On the Waterfront* (written by Budd Schulberg) Terry (Marlon Brando) believes he can sit on the fence and not choose between what is morally right or wrong. But he struggles with this all through the film and in the end he has to choose to do what is right.

What does she want?

Every character has a goal, but your central character's goal is the linchpin that holds your script together. It may be something reasonably achievable or small at the start, such as getting a particular job or organising an event. If so, as she pursues this 'smaller' goal, it will most likely grow into a goal with a far higher stake; possibly even life or death or saving the world.

For example, let's say her initial goal is to organise a conference on the environment. While doing this, however, she uncovers what appears to be a minor ethics breach. It might seem like a small thing to unveil but perhaps her determination to uncover the truth, even when advised not to do so, leads to a suspicion of corruption that spreads beyond the company, to the government, governments or agencies abroad and so on. Continuing to investigate who is behind this could have far-reaching consequences, depending on what is at stake for them if they are uncovered.

Alternatively, her goal may be clear from the start, such as robbing a bank, taking over the world or saving Earth from an alien invasion/ climate change.

Whatever route you choose, your readers need to understand your central character's goal and what is at stake so that they can judge whether she is succeeding or failing.

What is her motivation?

What is driving your central character to pursue her goal for as long as she does; to go as far as she will go and risk as much as she will risk? For your readers to empathise with her, they must understand her reasoning (and private emotional need), not just the external action she takes to achieve her goal.

Her motivation is often connected to the stakes and can be positive or negative. For example, *I want to be rich or I don't want to be poor; I don't like being lied to, so I want to know the truth or my reputation is all I have and I want it back.*

Again, the roots of her motivation stem from her backstory.

As was touched on in Chapter 3, provided readers understand what drives her to go further in pursuit of her goal than most people would, your central character becomes heroic, courageous and we want her to succeed.

If we don't understand her motivation, she seems foolish or selfish. The story becomes ridiculous and unbelievable and we pull back.

Alternatives to the classic protagonist

It is undoubtedly easier to tell a story when the central character drives the action. She makes things happen, finds the energy to keep trying and to make mistakes that lead to further conflict. That's why it's the norm.

You can tweak and twist the norm so it feels different and edgier, or you can use an alternative central character. There are risks involved regarding reader and, later, viewer engagement with your story if you opt for a central character who doesn't drive the action in the traditional sense so if you go that alternative route, make sure that the character you develop works *for* you and your story, not against.

The anti-hero

The anti-hero is the ultimate outsider; driven not by virtue but possibly by rebellion, danger or self-interest. She may even be the person we would be, if we had the nerve, or someone who behaves as we wish we could. This allows us to empathise or sympathise with her, even if it is uncomfortable or voyeuristic.

But if you have a central character who is severely dislikeable, how do you introduce her to us without us recoiling or choosing to read a different script? The trick is in the detail and the darkness of your story-world.

Take Travis Bickle (Robert de Niro) in *Taxi Driver,* written by Paul Schrader. This increasingly dangerous and psychotic taxi driver is pretty much *the* anti-hero and yet we end up rooting for him. Part of this is because the world in which he lives is a hundred times worse than he is. In *this* world, he is the good guy since he's trying to rescue the child prostitute, Iris (Jodie Foster) from her pimp.

Now let's look at the detail. The film opens with a diversion, the whole assassination subplot. This makes us curious about Bickle and interested in what will happen next. By the time the film kicks off, we should be intrigued enough to stay with him.

Melvin Udall in *As Good As It Gets* is homophobic, self-centred, selfish, racist *and* he has severe Obsessive Compulsive Disorder. But look at how the film opens. First the older neighbour's reaction to seeing Udall makes us laugh. She goes from happy and positive to scowling and swearing – and we haven't even seen him yet!

Then we watch his doomed attempt to negotiate with the tiny dog about to wee in the corridor. We cringe with him when the dog wees as he's holding him, possibly relate to his disgust and we laugh (guiltily?) when he puts the dog down the garbage chute because it takes us by surprise. The mis-quote from the Sinatra song is the icing on the cake: "*This is New York. If you can make it here, you can make it anywhere*".

Notice, apart from his gloves and his disgust at a dog weeing indoors, we haven't seen his OCD yet. The writer has also chosen the keep his homophobia back from our introduction to him.

Now look at some of the other choices the writer made in the creation of Udall.

First off, he writes hugely successful romance novels. Udall writes about love! That's a conscious choice. How much more clichéd would it have been if he wrote horror, dark twisted poetry or highbrow literary fiction? But it *is* a love story, hence the choice of genre.

That it is a love story seems incredible when you see Udall both in his own habitat and in public. To be credible, his change of character has to be incremental. It has to at least begin with Udall acting in his own interest, trying to remove obstacles to his goal of being able to continue his routine in the way that suits him best.

Take the scene in the restaurant. His goal in the scene is to have 'his' waitress, Carol serving him breakfast as she always does. Look at the difference between how Carol manages him and the fear (or loathing) he invokes in the other staff.

It is only because he wants Carol back serving him in the restaurant that he helps find and fund expert medical treatment for her son. So his 'good deed' comes from selfish motives that are entirely real. Meanwhile, the writer is creating a journey for Udall which will show us he is capable of change.

It begins when he is forced to care for the dog owned by Simon (Greg Kinnear), the gay neighbour he was so homophobic and nasty to at the start of the film. Udall falls for the dog, almost reluctantly and we realise he is capable of feelings. The dog transfers his loyalty to Udall but when this tears Simon apart, Udall reveals that his trick is to hide rashers in his pocket. He has listened to Simon's pain and tried to relieve it. Empathy, even if some of the motivation may come from discomfort or guilt. Now we see he can change.

The skill is in the detail:

- How you build your anti-hero from the ground up and out.
- How different she is to the world around her.
- How you build in the potential for (credible) change.

Then, when she changes, even slightly, we cheer.

Passive characters

It's difficult to relate to passive characters. They do little, are not driven to act and tend to wait for things to happen. 'Cool', for example, is not a helpful trait in a central character unless it somehow also drives her to act and react; maybe because her reputation for coolness is under threat.

The other danger of having a passive character as your lead is that the characters around them who do act will become far more interesting. This may skew your story in a direction you hadn't intended, leave your readers feeling the script is unfocussed or that the emotional impact it could have had is dispersed too broadly and away from your protagonist.

For a passive character to work as the central character, the world must be whirling. Then standing still in the eye of the storm may be seen as heroic.

> TIP: While scripts tend to be linear, action leading to reaction, screenwriting isn't. So, while you develop your characters, write up any and all scene ideas, scene fragments, elements of the story, lines of dialogue, images that come to you. Regardless of whether they seem logical or out of place in your story. They may turn out to be the key to something crucially important in your story.

Exercises

1. The diary

Write a diary in the voice of your central character from the moment your script starts. Let her describe how she experiences or perceives or reacts to key events in your story. It may throw up lines of dialogue, scenes you hadn't conceived of, locations, characters, perspective that can be invaluable. You're also bringing her voice directly and intimately to life.

If time is limited, take an event in your story or a moment after something has happened and let her write about this.

2. Beyond the questionnaire

Take the questionnaire in Chapter 3 and if you haven't already, interrogate your central character specifically. What if she doesn't answer honestly? What elements of her past would she recognise as having had an impact on her? Which ones would she deny?

Imagine you are interviewing her for a job or questioning her about something that happened in your story, how would she describe it or explain her role? Would she lie or simply see it differently?

3. The personal listography

- What five things make her happy?
- What five things make her sad?
- What are her three favourite words?
- Her two favourite colours?
- Her favourite TV shows/ films/ forms of entertainment?

You get the idea. Now add lists of things that are entirely off the wall as well as things that relevant to your theme or the story. You'll be surprised at what they throw up.

5. Populating Your Script: Choosing Your Cast

"I love Feydeau's one rule of playwriting. Character A: My life is perfect so long as I don't see Character B. Knock knock. Enter Character B."

— John Guare

Having established the dramatic question at the heart of your story and chosen your central character, it's time to populate both sides of the equation with people and then, in Chapter 6, we can get onto plotting.

The antagonist

The antagonist is the most important of your supporting cast. She's generally familiar with your central character's desires, but likely to be more familiar with having these desires thwarted. Arguably, that's what feeds her dark, destructive side.

A lot of films get their power and drama from the antagonist. We love to know who to hate. Look at *Michael Collins*, written by Neil Jordan. At the start, it's Collins (Liam Neeson) and company versus the British Empire. An empire is too big to be satisfying as an antagonist, so Jordan uses a series of different antagonists in turn, each of them increasing the stakes enormously until Ireland signs the treaty with Britain.

In the second half, following the treaty and on into the Civil War, it becomes Collins versus de Valera (Alan Rickman). It could be a film in two parts if it wasn't for the fact that the tension is there between them from the very start when the rebels are lined up following the Easter Rising. Their leaders are identified, including the severely wounded James Connolly who is dragged away. As Collins pushes out of the ranks, wanting to act in his defence, de Valera restrains him. Collins asks what they do now and de Valera tells him, "We wait".

The potential for the eventual antagonism that explodes later is planted: the man of action who feels deeply versus his leader, the pragmatist or politician who intellectualises the struggle. They have fundamentally different natures and value systems.

Even if Collins refuses to acknowledge it, this conflict is seeded in every scene they play together, which makes it feel entirely credible and a much more satisfying narrative when they end up pitted against each other.

You can choose to initially reveal that there is opposition or where it is coming from without necessarily identifying the individual who is ultimately behind it. The antagonism still needs to feel tangible – for example, through minions sent to do her dirty work or obstacles created by the antagonist – even if it is only as we get closer to the source that we realise who is masterminding it and how dangerous or powerful she actually is.

Role of your antagonist

Antagonists can be the most satisfying and interesting characters to write. They often provide the drama and conflict in a way that readers and audiences can literally feel. This makes it personal which, in turn, creates genuine anxiety and fear for the safety of your central character.

Your antagonist exists to show the conflict facing your central character, to highlight her weaknesses and deficiencies and her discomfort with these or with herself. Consider the film *Amadeus*. Our protagonist is Salieri (F. Murray Abraham) and he is in turmoil, his own worst enemy. Despite venerating Mozart's genius, he decides to destroy him because he believes God is mocking him through Mozart (Tom Hulce). His inability to make peace with himself is the source of the antagonism that drives him.

For the audience, this is best expressed visually by placing Mozart in opposition. That Mozart never realises he is the antagonist makes it even more powerful and tragic.

In many films, antagonists express the fears, frustrations and nightmares of their intended audience. It is possible to tell a story without one but it is trickier since you are relying on internal conflict. This can be hard to depict visually on screen. You need to plant the seeds of this conflict within your central character and make sure we understand them. Then it makes sense when your protagonist self-destructs.

The same steps go into developing your antagonist as your protagonist. Both have power and equally strong story purpose so you need to know them inside out.

Motivation

Let the antagonist's motivation be as strong as that of your central character so that they are worthy and exciting opponents. If you want to strengthen your antagonist, make her a representative of the world. Let the world of your story support her basic values so that the antagonist is the 'normal' one. She therefore has more power, access to knowledge and information and support from the world within which your central character struggles.

They need to be well-matched in terms of strength, even if your central character doesn't realise this until the end of your second act (See Chapter 9) or your central character has some secret strength/ weapon.

The stronger the antagonist is, the stronger your central character will have to be to overcome the odds stacked against her.

Personality

Since shades of grey are far more interesting than characters who are black or white, why not let your antagonist be charismatic, electric, with at least one admirable quality so we don't dismiss her as a clichéd 'bad guy'? It may even be that she doesn't intend to destroy your central character; she simply has a different agenda. This will make her defeat more provocative.

One fatal flaw

Your antagonist needs one flaw that will allow your initially less powerful central character to eventually win. For example, your antagonist is a violent enforcer who will do anything to prevent her young daughter from knowing what she does. Her weakness could be as simple as an allergy that your central character discovers and use to swing the odds in her favour at a crucial moment or it could be her desire to protect her daughter at all costs. It could be the negative way she treats the people who work for her or the arrogance and self-belief that leads her to treat her 'underlings' this way.

Make sure it isn't arbitrary

To work for you and your story, it must be credible and it must tie into the story. An irrational hatred of dogs could be interesting in a story about animal rights or a rom-com in which she pursues a romantic partner (for financial gain, rather than love) who happens to own a puppy farm.

> TIP: It can be very effective to stagger revelations about your antagonist. (See Chapter 5 on handling exposition.)

Secondary characters

Secondary characters are in your script to:

- Serve story purpose
- Show the character and personality of your central character.

Time and pages are limited, so each of your secondary characters must earn her place in your narrative. How can you assess who you really need in order to tell your story effectively?

- Each of your characters should have her own individual goal. Their goals tend to either be in conflict with your central character's goal or they want to help her achieve it. Each character's motivation is unique to her and it may not be the one you'd expect.

- Since nothing is black and white, in life or on the screen, your characters shouldn't be. However, secondary characters do have a singular, more clarified function in your story and so often end up appearing far more purposeful.

- All characters interact with each other. They all have an attitude towards or opinion of each other. Kindly, antagonistic or indifferent, nobody is neutral. Neutral leads to fluffy scenes where nothing actually happens.

By interacting with your central character, your secondary characters allow (and help) her to express her thoughts, desires, values, plans and show us why conflict is inevitable. They help show us that your central character is in conflict with herself, with the world and that her goal is difficult to achieve.

Just because we won't get to spend as much time with them is no excuse for them to be bland, unless their blandness is a character trait, of course! So ask them the questions. Dig into their biographies, look at their lives now and ask them what they want. What makes them interesting or conflicted? How do they feel about the central character, the antagonist, each other?

> TIP: It is often easier to write secondary characters. There may even be an inbuilt temptation in us all to overwrite them because there isn't as much at stake, so we can relax and have fun with them! Be careful not to let them overshadow your main characters.

Exercise:

1. The antagonist, some questions to ask:

- What's your antagonist's backstory?
- What is her motive, her goal, her emotional need and weakness or flaw?

- Has she met your central character before and if so, how/when/why? Is there residual business between them that was never dealt with?
- If only one of them remembers their (moment of) shared backstory, what if the antagonist appears, at first, to be an ally of some sort?
- Why have they come into each other's orbit now?
- Do either of them even realise they are in opposition? If not, when will they know?
- If your antagonist were telling the story of your film, what would be her perspective on events? On the central character?
- What would life have been like if your central character had never met the antagonist?

2. Secondary and support characters

Every character should have a distinct goal and purpose in the script. Take each one and ask them the following two questions.

- What is her goal or role in the story?

If two have a similar goal, could you merge them? Are there any characters you could lose or conflate without their loss changing the story adversely?

- What is their relationship with the central character? Are they only there to illustrate the backstory of your central character or have you added extra characters simply to make the plotting easier?

You only have room for four to six main characters. There may not be room for several friends and allies. To make sure they all have a distinct role, write down three main traits each of them have that will affect the storyline or impact upon your central character achieving her goal.

Stories based on real events are the hardest when it comes to cutting down on characters but readers can't relate to a vast array, whether the characters are worthy or despicable. If readers get confused, they may disengage from your story. So, if a character exists only to supply a piece of information or force your character to react, can you use another existing character instead?

3. Interrogation

Write five to ten questions you would love to ask someone you didn't know. Think of questions to do with the mind, with the heart and with physical needs, desire and fears. For example, what issues are important to them, what do they care about, who or what turns them on? Try these out on some of the characters you are thinking of using in your screenplay.

> TIP: Central characters tend to have a similar viewpoint to that of the writer, even if it can take each of them the length of their film to acknowledge this truth! This means they will often be at odds with the world in which they exist. So, when casting secondary characters, look for people with points of view that will be in conflict with or supportive of your central character, in order to highlight the dilemma she is in.

4. The Diary

You did this for your central character, now let your other main characters write their own versions of what happened to them during their time in your story. Their points of view may be skewed, biased or just plain 'wrong'. That is their value to you as a storyteller.

Not only can this exercise force you to see the world from several perspectives, but it can be a goldmine. Tiny details or phrases or observations or ideas for how a scene might play may make their way into the script and add power to your story.

> TIP: If you end up not using some of this character work, put it in a file marked 'Character'. There will be times in the future when you're stuck and need to make a character more interesting fast. One of

those traits or a snippet of backstory you didn't use in this script may be the breakthrough you need then.

5. Relationship Arc

I first saw this technique in a series' 'bible' for writers and it seemed a very clear way to capture the emotional world of the story.[1] Having decided on your main cast, do a relationship circle for your characters, with a line linking each one to all the others. On top of each linking line write how one character feels about the other. Underneath, write how the other feels, with an arrow indicating direction. Now you have a visual map of how your cast interconnects within your story

If you have more to write, have little feeder lines outwards, maybe adding how each character believes she is perceived by the other, how long they have known each other, the one thing they admire or hate about the other, etc.

This is your world and everyone in it has an attitude to and opinion on everyone else. What is each character's relationship to other characters and especially your central character?

This might lead to questions such as:

- Would it be interesting to have an antagonist who believes she is helping your central character to make the right choice?
- An ally who turns out to be working for the other side?
- Are there connections here that are unacknowledged, secret or unknown?

TIP: How a character perceives herself to be seen by other characters might not be how she is seen in reality. Similarly, how we see ourselves can be very different from how others see us. This can be useful in generating misunderstandings, conflict and action.

---

[1] (A 'bible' in this case is the document that contains all the information a writer working on the series would need to know about the world and the characters in order to write a script that would fit the style and tone of the series.)

6: Into The Depths: Plotting The Story

"The King dies and then the Queen dies is story. The King dies and then the Queen dies from grief is plot."

– E.M. Forster

You have your characters, you have your idea. Before I dive into structure, I want you to start excavating the key moments you need to tell your story.

This is the time to be open to possibilities. Any idea comes with a number of key moments or events and you need to be open to finding more interesting ways to reach or to reveal these moments.

Let's say you know that your central character's mother will die because this will cause her to question herself and her journey. How her mother dies, how and when your central character finds out, what happens leading up to it, the emotional impact you want the discovery to have on your central character and your readers, whether it's a surprise or the reader knows before your central character…

All of these choices can change where you place her mother's death in the timeline, when it is discovered and how much impact it has on your central storyline and character – but also on your subplots if you have any.

Structure versus plot

Structure is the blueprint of how you intend people to react to your film, but plot is how you design the ride. Plot creates pace and momentum. It is the arrangement of information and events to make your screenplay exciting to read and it is how you make readers feel what you want them to feel.

As such, plot primarily puts pressure on your central character to act and works through the principles of suspense and surprise. All the way through your screenplay, you pique our curiosity and subvert our expectations. You present or withhold information. You plant information that we won't even realise the value of until further down the line.

For example:

- You write a scene in which Jane says she hasn't seen Meg for months. As soon as she hangs up, Meg walks out from the room behind her in a bath towel.
- Your central character identifies a dead woman as her mother. Later we discover this woman wasn't her mother at all.

In effect, you speed the ride up, slow it down or have it explode under us.

Opening the story up

Before we look at formula, let's be creative. Sticking with the 'ride' analogy, wouldn't you prefer to imagine all the fairground rides you could design before you sat down and worked out the mechanical logistics or whether they would be feasible in reality?

Let's say your central character's friend Alice slips an envelope into her pocket. We later discover it's payment for information she gave to the antagonist about your central character.

Her reasons may be:

- She believes she is doing this in the central character's best interest
- She hates the central character (why?) but has concealed it for monetary gain
- She's a spy, purely doing her job – but maybe she has started to care and might be (or become) a double agent
- She's being blackmailed or has history with the antagonist

When you're plotting your story, you decide how much of her motivation the reader will know. This will have an effect on how the revelation of her betrayal plays for us. You also decide when we find out about the payment, whether we know before your central character, whether and when we discover Alice's motivation.

Plotting is fun

Every decision opens up options for your story.

Considering all the possibilities can be a little unsettling because, as you can see with the example above, every decision you explore could lead you and your story in a different direction. It's up to you to choose the most interesting and useful option for your story, not necessarily the easiest.

For example, what will your central character do when she discovers Alice's betrayal? What has Alice already revealed to the antagonist that will work against the central character achieving her goal? Is it possible that Alice could be playing both sides off against each other or that the central character will be able to play Alice off against the antagonist?

Plot points

Plot points are important moments in your story when the dynamic shifts. They are based on or caused by obstacles that your central character has to overcome. Put more simply, each plot point is a moment/ event/ revelation/ decision that *has* to happen for your story to be told dramatically.

Right now, I want you to brainstorm as many obstacles as you can find to place between your character's goal and her success or failure. It is by forcing your central character to respond to obstacles that you create drama and conflict, that you create emotion on screen.

Once you have all your choices, you can answer the question, *"What will work best for my screenplay?"*

Early plot points

Early plot points open up the story. At this stage, every choice your central character makes will lead to different options, obstacles, events and consequences. She will always make the wrong decision, even if it doesn't appear to be so (at least to her) at the time.

As such, being the storyteller, you choose obstacles and events that will help your plot, generally by making life more difficult for your central character on a physical, emotional, mental or practical level. With each decision she makes, your central character (often unknowingly) increases the jeopardy she faces and keeps the story rolling.

Notably, if the option she chooses makes life a little better for a while, it will definitely backfire later. For example, let's say your central character decides to engage in a romantic relationship with Alice. It's against her initial best instincts and might even be the first time she decides to trust someone for decades. And she trusts Alice deeply. It's the best relationship she has ever had and she can't believe her luck.

In this scenario, Alice's betrayal will be all the more disruptive and destructive.

Later plot points

By reducing options, later plot points help focus the story. They force your central character to focus on what she needs to do to resolve the crisis and answer the dramatic question. For example, let's take the discovery by your central character that Alice is working for the antagonist. This knowledge leaves her with several choices:

- She can use this information, without revealing to Alice that she knows Alice is working for the antagonist
- Reassess her actions to date based on this knowledge and change her plan of action going forward
- Force, blackmail or trick Alice to work for her
- Set Alice up in order to find more out by how she responds/ where she goes
- Force Alice to reveal what she knows or what the antagonist knows

However, if the discovery of the betrayal happens late in the script, her choices will be more stark since Alice will have had time to reveal more to the antagonist. As a result, there is more at stake for your central character and she is at her most vulnerable because time is running out.

If she doesn't make the right choice now, she will be in an even worse place than she has been yet and will have no chance of success.

Plot pillars

Key plot points are called **pillars**. You recognise them because the ending of your story would be entirely different if any were taken out or changed. As such, they are critical moments in your story that absolutely have to happen. They yield surprise, increase tension, make the audience anxious and hook us into the story.

We talk in plotting about the 'height' of plot pillars. Height refers to the level of jeopardy or what is at stake as a result of these moments. This is calculated based on how you believe your readers will react and how bad the consequences are for your central character.

The greater the **jeopardy** they cause, the higher and more important the pillars become. As such, each needs to be higher than the last. There has to be more at stake, more to lose.

Turning points

Certain of these pillars are **turning points** because they turn the action in an unexpected and different direction. These are critical moments for your central character, even if she doesn't realise it. She is forced to act or make a decision that changes everything. Forever.

There are many different types of turning points, such as barriers, discoveries, complications, reversals and they all behave exactly as they sound.

A barrier may be when your character goes to access information on a computer and discovers she has been locked out of the system.

A complication might be that the information she accesses suggests that the person she was investigating isn't who she thinks it is, is actually also a victim or that what she was investigating is not as simple to unravel as she thought.

A reversal could be that the memory key she thought had information she needed contains a virus instead that destroys all the evidence she had gathered.

A discovery might be when she finds that envelope from the antagonist in the pocket of her friend and ally, Alice.

Turning points generally end a particular sequence of events. Not only should they change the story's direction and raise the central question again – *will your central character succeed in her goal?* –, they should also demand a commitment or decision from her.

While they can happen at any stage they *must* happen at the end of Act 1 and Act 2. While we will go into more detail in the following chapters on three-act structure, the logic of these two essential turning points is worth looking at now in the context of the overall plot.

Turning Points 1 and 2

As with all early plot points, **Turning Point 1** opens up options for your central character. The story could go anywhere depending on the choice she makes. If she discovers that her friend Alice is working for the antagonist now, for example, there are several options open to her. Each will lead the story and her plan of action in a different direction.

Alternatively, **Turning Point 2** narrows the options available. What if she discovers that her ally and friend, Alice IS the antagonist? Wouldn't that reduce the options open to her dramatically? She now realises, suddenly, that she is more vulnerable than she believed she was, increasing the tension for the reader. Time is running out and she has very few options.

With both turning points, the decision your central character makes precipitates the end of the act and increases the stakes enormously.

> TIP: Turning points can be intriguing or unpredictable, but they have to be credible.

Think big

Right now, you want to find as many plot points within your story as you can. Weeding out can happen later when you structure your screenplay but don't, please don't reduce your options now out of lack of confidence or a fear that you are being melodramatic.

Anything can happen.

This is your story and unless you let it fly at this stage, you could be limiting the ideas you come up with and might miss out on some unique and wonderful options. Also, even if you don't use certain plot points or interesting obstacles in your final screenplay, some element of these moments or events may end up adding bite or colour to another scene or telling you something useful about character that you can use elsewhere in the script.

The bigger picture

Once you have your plot pillars, line them up. The pattern you end up with is a useful visual map that can help you to not get lost when you're writing the actual script. Some of your plot points have a clear and natural order but if you're uncertain, now is the time to move them around and see which points you really need to include. (See **Exercise**, below)

Some will clog the story down because they're not adding anything new to the story while others might make it move too fast by revealing too much too soon. Sometimes the solution is to leave them out, for now. Other times, it's a matter of placing them elsewhere, merging several together or adding additional character/ story information.

For example, when do you reveal that your central character's friend, Alice, is working against her? The position of this plot point will determine how important it is to the story and to your central character's quest. Where it happens and how may also be critical. If it happens in a public place, when she's alone or when Alice is in the same room will change how she can or can't react.

Filling in the gaps

The second point to be aware of is that, while plot pillars are moments in your story that cannot be changed, the scene or sequence of scenes preceding it absolutely can be. You choose what we see and hear dramatically in the minutes leading up to your crucial scene.

- What do we need to know before each plot point?
- What do you need to hold back?

Let's take that scene where your central character discovers Alice's betrayal. What happens immediately before this discovery and in the sequence of scenes leading up to it will have an impact on how powerful the reveal will be, both in terms of plot but also of emotional impact on your central character and the reader.

This is regardless of whether the events in these preceding scenes may or may not involve Alice.

Questions to ask:

- What do you want us to know before we find out about Alice's betrayal?
- How much will you choose to reveal to your reader in relation to Alice's motivation, to her relationship and history with your central character and with the antagonist?
- How much has Alice revealed or has she refused to reveal?
- Have we even seen Alice with the antagonist or is this a total surprise to us too?

Take *In The Name Of The Father*. Gerry Conlon is arrested in Belfast. He's flush with money and has no alibi for the night of the bombing, as is necessary for his arrest. That's your plot pillar.

In the scenes preceding it, Gerry and Paul Hill have to leave the squat and therefore have no convincing alibi for the night. They meet up with Charlie Bourke (Joe McPartland), the tramp who will (eventually) be their alibi.

Gerry gives him their last coins. They find keys to a hooker's apartment. Gerry decides to go inside and accidentally finds a large amount of cash.

Those are the choices the writer made. The duo could have found money lost in a public or private space, thieved it or begged. (Borrowing might have given them an alibi.) The hooker's apartment could have been an open car, a family home, a business, a train station, an ATM with cash left in it.

In other words, it was essential to the internal logic of your plot that Gerry was back in Belfast, flush with money he couldn't explain and with no alibi for the night but there were any number of options regarding how these elements were dramatically achieved.

In a screenplay, everything leads to or has an impact on something or someone else. Even if it feels random to the characters, it isn't in your narrative.

In this case, luck (the dropped keys) and character (Gerry opting to use the keys, messing around and finding the money accidentally but then stealing it) helps Gerry and Paul. They can now sleep in a hotel, buy new clothes and Gerry can afford to visit Belfast.

It works against them in that it leads to their incarceration.

> TIP: If you're feeling stuck when looking for plot points to keep your script building, play with the idea of the best and worst thing that can happen to your characters.

Sequencing

Sequences are blocks of action, linked by the same purpose and/ or idea. They have their own mini-storyline and if you took them out of the film, individually they would feel like short films.

Each sequence will have a beginning, middle and end, much as the three-act itself does (See chapters 7-9), while telling a simpler story. A feature film can be built using a series of such sequences. In addition, they may be action or event-based. For example, the opening riot sequence in *In The Name Of The Father* or the christening sequence in *The Godfather Part II* (written by Francis Ford Coppola and Mario Puzo).

Exercise

Finding your plot points

Step 1: Brainstorm all the obstacles you can put in the path of your central character, based on everything you know or don't yet know and what you could do to your character using the people and the world around her. Any of these may become critical plot pillars, helping you to structure your story.

- If she has a fear of the colour red, use it.
- If she has a fear of heights, use it.
- How badly does the antagonist want to stop her and why? Use that.

Step 2: Having listed them, do a little dance/ break open a bar of chocolate. Congratulate yourself. Progress has been made.

Step 3: Put your obstacles in order, ranging in how much trouble they will cause for your central character. Which ones will have the most effect on the character and your readers? Do they all achieve something different?

Step 4: Start imagining the pieces in between.

Ask yourself, how can I dramatise the action leading up to this point? Be creative and see where your imagination takes you; these plot points are only on the page and can be jettisoned but may reveal options you hadn't considered before.

7: Structure: the Three-Act Formula

"Scripts are what matter. If you get the foundations right and then you get the right ingredients on top, you stand a shot… but if you get those foundations wrong, then you absolutely don't stand a shot. It's very rare – almost never – that a good film gets made from a bad screenplay."

– Tim Bevan

Now you have the bones, it's time to build your story into a logical, cohesive and irresistible script. In theory, it's not that hard. 'All' you have to do is grab and hook your audience, make us care about your central character and throw her over the edge into chaos. The trick then is to keep complicating her world, making it nearly impossible for her to achieve her goal, so you keep your readers emotionally involved.

Within the average hundred-page script, the number of scenes varies. An action movie might have two hundred and twenty scenes while a rom-com or character-driven script might have only one hundred and sixty. Since a single paragraph of action could last as much as several minutes on screen, dialogue-heavy pages run faster but overall it's accepted that each properly formatted page (see Chapter 16) of a screenplay is 1-1.5 minutes of screen time.

I'm only giving you this now so that you have a sense of the exciting amount of material you have to play with when you're weaving your story.

~ ~ ~

Some people love structure, some hate it. For me, it's a mixture of both. I do find it difficult with some stories but once I have the structural outline airtight (ish!), I can have fun writing the script without worrying that I don't know where I'm heading or might get lost en route.

When it works, the structure you build should be invisible.

But it can feel daunting to structure something as large as a screenplay. To avoid this, we will look at how to do it in parts so that it feels less intimidating overall.

The first stage is to decide on the elements you need in your story for it to work. Chances are, by now, you've found many of them. The next stage is to put those elements in order, to build an outline of how your script will look. And remember, when you get this first draft done, you will have achieved an act of pure awesomeness.

Since this is your first script and the goal is to get pages down, I'm focussing here on the three-act structural formula so beloved by Hollywood. I loathe those generic films that appear on the big screens every year in which this formula is as visible as the clichéd stories it holds together. But screenplays need structure and, if you look at it closely, the three-act formula, at its loosest and most pure, is the oldest form of storytelling.

It is hard for readers and the general audience to connect with a series of random scenes, for example; if it doesn't satisfy them emotionally, that can be a waste of great material.

Following the rules?

As for cravenly following all the 'rules', what I would suggest is that before you challenge the rules that sustain the film industry's favourite formula, you need to understand them. Then, if you decide to follow your own structural format, you know why you're breaking the rules, what you risk by doing so and what you hope to gain.

The other key formula I use is The Hero's Journey. I generally use it in tandem with the three-act formula, not only because I prefer the emotional language of the terms belonging to the Hero's Journey but also because they complement each other.

Beginning, middle and end

The first and most basic piece of information you need to know about the three-act formula is that everything is balanced. All three-acts are calibrated for stability, in a way that can seem mechanical but is basically logical.

You can effectively slice up your script into four quarters, like a pie: Act 1 is a quarter of the script, Act 2 is the next two quarters and Act 3 is the final quarter. Therefore, with some flexibility, in a hundred-page script, Act 1 is roughly twenty-five pages long, Act 2 is fifty and Act 3 is twenty-five pages pages; in a sixty page TV script, they will be fifteen, thirty and fifteen. Approximately – it's not an exact science!

In essence:

Act 1 is set-up.

Act 2 is conflict and confrontation.

Act 3 is resolution and redemption.

This is why they have to be balanced. If you take fifty pages to set-up your story, you only have fifty left in which to tell your story.

So far, so simple: beginning, middle, end.

~~~

To make it as easy as possible to absorb what you need, I've broken my interpretation of the three-act formula into three chapters. First up – and taking the most space – is Act 1. This is where the majority of problems lie in a script when it isn't working. If you put the work into the first 25 pages of your feature script, as well as into developing character and story, you can avoid many of these.

Then we will move into Act 2 and 3 and in Chapter 10 we will look at advantages, disadvantages and, briefly, some alternatives.

Exercise

1. Read the first ten pages of five scripts. Write down when and how you discover the central character. What page was it on? What was she doing? What impact or impression did she give you? Did you care yet? What did the writer do to hook you into the story? How did she introduce the world? Was it credible?

2. Now read the next twenty pages of two scripts: your favourite one and the one you found least gripping. This time, you're looking to see what the writer did to pull you further in. At what point did you start really caring about the central character, or lose interest?

If the story hadn't hooked you in the first ten minutes, did this change? If so, note the moment when it changed. What happened, how did the writer do this?

8: Act 1: The Set-up

"If your head doesn't hurt, you're not working hard enough!"
                    – advice given at a comedy writing workshop

Let's look at how Act 1 sets up your story. It's the foundation for all that follows. If it is to pull us in and make sure that we keep turning the pages for the next ninety minutes or so, Act 1 has to be gripping or intriguing.

The first ten minutes

These first ten to twelve pages are critical. This is based on the conventional wisdom that viewers of the finished film will make up their minds whether the film is worth the effort within ten minutes.

However, at script stage, development executives and producers may decide within three pages, if not one. I believe that Robert Towne, the writer of *Chinatown*, claimed that if the last ten minutes are brilliant, the audience will forgive you the rest.

In your script, let's aim for both!

Either way, your set-up needs to begin immediately or directly after an opening scene or sequence that has piqued our interest.

The opening image or sequence

As I've already said, this needs to be visual and intriguing. You want to engage us emotionally or intellectually. Generally, it will have something to do with story/ theme, give us a hint or clue as to what your story will be about and the genre/ tone to expect.

There are any number of ways in which you can achieve this. You might introduce us to an interesting world, an image that shocks us, a scene that intrigues. For example, in *Witness* (written by William Kelley, Pamela Wallace and Earl W Wallace) we open in the Amish community, a world of which most of us have no experience. Rachel (Kelly McGillis) leaves to visit her sister. A delayed train means her son Samuel witnesses the murder which propels them into the gritty criminal world of Detective John Book (Harrison Ford) and the story 'proper' begins.

Similarly, in *The Truman Show* (written by Andrew Niccol), we see Truman (Jim Carrey) talking to himself in the bathroom mirror on an average morning; but this is interspersed with interview snippets. Christof, the creator (Ed Harris), Truman's wife, Meryl (Laura Linney) and his best friend, Marlon (Noah Emmerich) all tell us about the show. We know within minutes that Truman's world is a TV show and that he is the only innocent.

In *Blade Runner (*written by Hampton Fancher and David Peoples, based on Philip K Dick's novel, *Do Androids Dream of Electric Sheep?*), we open with a skyline not dissimilar to an extreme version of Los Angeles, the first striking difference being the spikes of flame as excess gas is burnt off into the atmosphere.

Your character

Introduce your central character as soon as possible. As readers and viewers, we like to know whose story we are following. Ideally, she will be doing something that makes her memorable. Unique.

Think of when we meet Udall in *As Good As It Gets*: he's putting a tiny dog down a garbage chute. In the coming-of-age comedy *Juno (*written by Diablo Cody), Juno McGuff (Ellen Page) is ruminating about a lounge set left on a front lawn while drinking litres of Sunny D.

The ordinary world or status quo

This is your central character's world. Make us believe in it. Introduce whatever element(s) of her life/ persona that you will put in jeopardy in Act 1, however subliminally. Let us see how she feels about herself, her life and her emotional need, even if she doesn't really admit this need to herself.

It's not enough for her world to be contemporary or based on a true life story, it must be consistent in its details to be an authentic and convincing fictional reality. In other words, if it feels true to itself, we will believe in it. Similarly, if you're creating a fictional or fantasy world, you write the rules and then abide by them throughout the film.

Take, for example, *Alien*, written by Dan O'Bannon. We are in outer space but all the astronauts are concerned with when they are woken up is whether they will they get extra pay for this unscheduled stop? They're in dungarees; they drink, smoke; little collectibles of life clutter the mess table.

Pieces of home.

They're like long distance truck drivers in space, so it feels both familiar and authentic, despite being in space.

Exposition

What do your readers need to know in Act 1 for them to get involved in the story you are spinning? Let us find this out and only this. Leave us wanting to know more. A heap of backstory on your central character, for example, isn't necessary here but if she has special characteristics that will eventually help or hinder her, it could be useful to get an idea of them or see them in action, even slightly.

Be very careful not to *tell* your readers the information you feel they need to know. For example, if you need to tell us that she was brought up by her grandfather, there must be a gazillion ways to let us know or suspect this without her saying, *"I was brought up by my grandfather".*

She might have memorabilia that are special to her from that time. Possibly, she uses old-fashioned phrases or has attitudes inherited from her grandfather that she hasn't shed. Yet. Maybe she acts in a particular way around elderly people – good or bad, depending on what her relationship was like with her grandfather. She might tell people they're lucky to have parents or be short-tempered with them when they moan about having to visit. She might have a walking stick by the front door. A lucky talisman. Maybe he's still around and a vital part of the story or she has his ashes on her mantelpiece in a ceramic vase shaped like a parrot.

And that's the thing. Once you work out what you want or need to reveal, you can look for a way to let your readers discover it through action, behaviour, reactions, dialogue, props or setting, etc. Brainstorm how this fragment of the story has affected your character's life so that you can find interesting ways to reveal it.

How important that revelation is will tell you whether you can reveal it within the fabric of another scene or whether it needs to be the point of a scene or sequence of events. For example, if your character is a marathon runner, it could be enough to show her running gear in the hall or her medals in the background. In a different story, we might learn through an argument at work because her boss has pulled her in when she needs the time to train.

In yet another story, it could be that she's injured and refusing to admit it, or that moment when her child claims that she loves running more than him because she's late collecting him from a birthday party.

Catalyst

Time to up the ante.

Something has to happen in your story that will force your central character to act. The catalyst is the first major plot point in your script. It can't be arbitrary, although it might seem so to your central character at the time. It must also happen on screen.

The audience has to know *this* is important.

The purpose of the catalyst is to push your central character to the brink. The decision she then makes will radically upset the balance in her life and thrust her into inevitable confrontation with the forces of antagonism.

In other words, when she acts, (**Turning Point 1**), *everything* changes.

Needs and desires

Ideally, the catalyst will arouse both conscious and unconscious needs and desires, hopefully in conflict. For example, in *Amadeus*, Salieri utterly adores Mozart's work. Mozart's wife, Stanzi (Elizabeth Berridge) brings her husband's work to Salieri behind his back so that he can be considered for an appointment. Her motive is pure: they need the money; Mozart is better at spending it than earning.

However, in the middle of the scene, she admits that Mozart never makes copies. Stanzi has no idea how important this information is and that's why the revelation works. Salieri now discovers that Mozart writes his perfect music without correction, as if taking dictation from God.

As a result, because he now feels personally slighted by God, he sets out to destroy God's 'instrument', Mozart while Stanzi is oblivious to the damage she has done.

What does the catalyst look like?

A catalyst tends to be action, often **a specific action, happening or event**. For example, in *The Player* (written by Michael Tolkin), the writer stalking the producer Griffin Mill (Tim Robbins) sends another card, this time threatening to kill him.

But it can also be dialogue: **something revealed or information received**, in whatever way works best for your story. For example, in *Witness*, Detective Book confides in his old mentor, Schaeffer (Josef Sommer) who tips off the murderer as to the identity of the witness.

Alternatively, you could build the catalyst up from **a series of small incidents** that add up to more. Maybe a phone ringing in the background or someone desperately trying to get in touch but your central character only reaches out when it's too late and that person is missing/ dead/ unable to talk because she has been threatened.

Then there's the **set-up and payoff** version which can work well. For example, in *Jaws*, (written by Peter Benchley and Carl Gottlieb) when the girl is taken by the shark but her body is found later.

What is consistent is that, generally, the solution (for your central character) appears to be an easy one. For example, in *The Player*, Studio Executive Mill decides to find the writer and offer to buy his script.

Without a catalyst, a script can meander and never quite get going.

TIP: If your central character refuses to act, the stakes will have to rise in order to force her to dive in. In other words, something else will have to happen that will leave her with no choice but to act. Thus, in *Star Wars* (written by George Lucas), when Luke (Mark Hamill) refuses to go and rescue Princess Leia, he returns home to discover that the Empire's stormtroopers have killed everyone. Now he wants to fight.

Where should it happen?

The catalyst happens when you're ready for it to happen within your first act. Every story is different. For example, in *On The Waterfront*, Terry unwittingly helps the mob kill an informer at two minutes in. In *Taxi Driver*, Iris jumps into the cab driven by Bickle, igniting his need to save her, twenty-seven minutes into the film.

But be careful. If you leave it too late, you will need a subplot to keep our attention. For example, Bickle's lunatic attempts at political assassination in *Taxi Driver*.

Turning point 1

Turning Point 1 is the evil twin of the catalyst. Nothing will ever be the same. If the catalyst introduced a problem, it also invoked in your central character the need to resolve this problem, leading to action that will make life so much worse than she can currently imagine.

This leaves us with the dramatic question, *Will she succeed or fail?* that will hold your script together and hook us as readers, *provided we care.*

The choice your central character makes now is generally related to her backstory. It appears to be the solution to her dilemma because it seems to answer the dramatic question that the catalyst raised. For a moment, therefore, it looks good, but it turns out your central character has made a mistake. Maybe she underestimated her adversary or the situation but it is an obvious wrong turn.

As such, Turning Point 1 signals the end of Act 1.

In *Witness*, for example, because he told Schaeffer about Samuel, Book now has to flee into the Amish community to protect the boy.

It's worth noting that your central character has no idea of how bad things are going to get. The choice she makes now may seem like the solution to all her current problems. In reality, it will make everything a whole lot worse. In *Amadeus*, Stanzi's revelation has turned Salieri into Mozart's mortal enemy. In *The Player*, Mill murders the wrong writer by accident and chooses to pretend it was a robbery. In *In Name Of The Father*, Gerry's theft of the cash from the hooker's apartment is the solution to their problem of having no money but because this is the night of the Guildford bombing, having a large amount of cash and no alibi make them key suspects for the bombing.

In *Chinatown*, private detective Gittes (Jack Nicholson) decides to find out who has set him up because he wants to know the answer. He has no idea who he is up against but even when things get rough, he doesn't consider backing down. Why? Because his reputation is important to him. It's all he has left, after what happened in Chinatown. We never learn much about that incident but it's a powerful motivation for him.

Once your central character has made her choice, she can never return to the 'ordinary world' unchanged. The stakes are now higher and will keep rising all through Act 2. Her decision will either destroy her or ultimately lead to salvation. Crucially, we now care because we have a better idea than she has of how difficult it will be for her to succeed.

Therefore we want her to succeed.

To summarise: what do you need in Act 1?

Bear in mind that theory is just that. Theory. It's the academic or analytical side of screenwriting. In practice all these elements may overlap, rules will be broken or crushed by the demands of a strong story or a strong individual writer's voice. That you draw us into the story and make sure we aren't confused or lost is the goal of Act 1.

You need:

- **An opening image/ sequence** that grabs our attention and in which something happens.
- **A central character** you introduce to us in a way we will remember.
- To establish **the status quo or ordinary world**. This world could be a relationship, a community, a family or a workplace. You need to show us what your central character stands to lose by showing us the world that will be changed forever by this story.
- **A hook.** Within ten minutes, you need to pull us in, to make us want to know what happens next.
- **Exposition.** Give us the information that we need to continue into Act 2.
- **A catalyst** that will change everything for your central character.
- **Turning Point 1.** When you character makes a decision as a result of the catalyst that will start the real story
- We will meet most if not all of **your principal characters** within the first 20 pages of your feature script. The confrontation lines are drawn. Not developed, possibly not clear, but the seeds have been planted.

Bearing in mind that several of these could be achieved in one scene or sequence, you may also have:

- **Subplot(s)**: The main subplot is often a love story, but all subplots generally reflect on some aspect of your overall story or theme. (See Chapter 9)
- **A mentor**: Someone who will to advise or help your central character, even if she (generally) doesn't realise the value of the advice or help yet.

Exercise

1. Starting Act 1

- Your story will begin in a specific setting, time and place. Where and when you start can be crucial. The question to ask is, *Why now? Why am I not starting this story a week later, an hour before?*

What would happen if you chose to start it in a different place?

- Very roughly, sketch out a sequence of scenes in which you start your script at two different points of time in the story: a week earlier and a week later.

2. Step outline

- Run through the checklist at the end of the chapter and see if you have the ingredients you need to do a step outline for Act 1.
- Line them all up and see what you else you need to find for this to hold together as your first act. Brainstorm options for linking the plot points you want to use.
- Summarise the scenes you have, one line apiece. Only describe how each of them moves the story or character on. You're only writing the information necessary to move your story forward.

This outline is purely about momentum and structure, ensuring that you have everything you need.

9: On With the Story: Acts 2 & 3

"There is no reason why challenging themes and engaging stories have to be mutually exclusive – in fact, each can fuel the other. As a filmmaker, I want to entertain people first and foremost. If out of that comes a greater awareness and understanding of a time or a circumstance, then the hope is that change can happen."

– Edward Zwick

If drama is conflict, Act 2 is when it really kicks off.

You enter Act 2 with all the important exposition done. Your readers have all the information they need to enjoy the ride. They know whose story it is and what her problem is. They care, at least slightly, for your central character. The trick now is to ensure that the conflict keeps building so that your readers care more and *need* her to succeed because of what or who she's up against.

For this to happen, each obstacle you place in your central character's path should be more difficult for her to overcome or, if easy to overcome, this success will backfire. Ideally, some of them are obstacles she could not have foreseen, thought would not happen or hoped she had avoided but the stakes have to keep rising.

As she pursues her goal, critically she makes friends and enemies while you heap complication upon complication until there seems to be no way she can succeed. It is the most exciting act, but it's also the longest and can feel unwieldy, so it's good to plan out what you want to do before diving in.

The stakes must increase in height

Stakes vary, depending on your central character, your story and where we are within it. This is why we focussed on obstacles before tackling structure. Story and character determine the '**height**' of each obstacle you place in her path and where you position it for maximum impact. You have any amount of potential obstacles but by now it should be clearer which ones will help you tell the story most effectively and powerfully.

Let's say you create a character whose unique flaw is a fear of women. She might find a room full of women harder to overcome than facing a team of guerrilla fighters down a dark lane at midnight in the rain with a broken leg – though, admittedly, probably only in a comedy.

In one story, a high stake might be the central character losing her driving licence, her hair, her lucky coin. In another, your stakes might include the risk or reality that her family will be kidnapped, that she will be found in possession of (planted?) drugs or that she will lose the use of the fingers on one hand.

Again, it's the cost to your central character of consequences that happen as a result that will determine their height as stakes.

> TIP: Keep your central character's goal and need to the forefront when thinking of obstacles. The obstacles she faces have to make it increasingly difficult for her to move forward as she had planned.

Mid Point

Half way through Act 2, it's useful to think of a Mid Point supporting the middle of the script. It stops Act 2 becoming unwieldy. Like your first turning point and catalyst, it is simply one of your key plot pillars.

Turning Point 2

At the end of Act 2, your central character is forced to face the mistake she made at the end of Act 1: the decision that had so many consequences. Now, she faces the truth. She must do this while dealing with her own internal weakness or flaw. This flaw has been holding her back, be it denial of a fear of flying, a need for control or her inability to ask for help.

This realisation only happens when things are worse than they have ever been and there may seem to be no way out. *Now* she realises that she should never have trusted this person or that, that the forces she was up against are far greater than she expected and, most importantly, that time is running out.

By the time readers get to this stage, they're emotionally exhausted. They've been through so much with your central character that there's a chance they could be indifferent to her fate. Having resolved her internal dilemma, she is now faced with the worst scenario possible and is forced to dig deep.

She has to do something special, something we would not be capable of doing to turn the scene around and spin the action in a new direction into Act 3.

Her new skill or strength can't be arbitrary

She can't suddenly discover a skill or strength of which there has been no hint to date and then retrospectively explain how it was there all along because of some event in their past. (See **backstory** below.) For example, in a very simplistic storyline, we have a 13-year-old being hunted by a sniper. (Let's not even try to explore the reasons why for now!) The SAS have failed to assassinate him, as have shooters in helicopters, the police, an assassin on her side, etc. Now your teen picks up a gun when nobody is looking and shoots the sniper with one perfect shot.

Then she explains that her parents were murdered when she was five and her grandfather took her to his farm and force-trained her to use every kind of weapon.

That's bad storytelling.

What you need to do is **foreshadow** that this skill is there, under the surface, to ensure that whatever she does in this scene makes sense for readers and for your eventual audience. It's an 'I told you so' moment that allows us to feel smug because we've seen and understood the clues, even if we only realise their significance now.

Let's say we've seen this child playing pool and accurately calibrating the angles of balls using the side of the table or watching a shootout on telly and commenting that it wouldn't have panned out that way, but nobody hears her because she's in a safe house and her minders are arguing or flirting or making coffee. What if she finds a gun in the apartment and picks it up the right way, freaking everyone out but nobody for one moment assumes she knows what she's doing?

I'm not saying any of these would work specifically. Depending on your characters and your story, there could be any number of tiny clues buried within scenes that would finally add up when we discover her skill with a gun.

We have already established that she will only be able to use this skill because she has confronted her own weakness or flaw. In this scenario, what might that flaw be and where has it come from? Was she was so traumatised by her time with her grandfather that she has been unable to touch a gun since? Or is it survivor guilt, a feeling that she should have died with her parents that means she won't handle guns because she doesn't want to be able to protect herself? In either case, maybe her protector has to die in this scene before she can act or she acts to protect someone else, younger than her?

Pushing this to an extreme, perhaps you've given her a backstory in which she accidentally shot her grandfather dead towards the end of his intensive training. Maybe he pushed her too hard and she reacted with violence and swore never to touch a gun again because she doesn't trust herself? Could she have blacked this from her mind until now?

The point is that you decide what her backstory is, the flaw or weakness and the strength or skill she has as a result. Foreshadow that she has this skill and then, when she overcomes her own weakness or flaw and is able to use this skill, it feels credible.

It also makes sense that she could only overcome her flaw in the face of the worst possible scenario, such as life or death, possibly of someone to whom she has grown close. Motivation to finally act could be love, fury, wanting it all to end, revenge, the need to protect... Again, that will come from her backstory.

What is important is that when she finally shoots the sniper, we may be surprised initially but we also believe she is capable of doing this now. Almost subliminally, we have been prepared so that your crucial revelatory scene works.

Your central character has just created Turning Point 2.

Role of backstory

Because of the issue of foreshadowing and redemption, your central character's backstory is crucial. As with the scenario above, you need to know what haunts her most, even if she is in denial of it. Then you make sure it turns up in your film script.

Her backstory can also suggest a fatal pattern, a tragic inevitability that she may fight against. Knowing what this is can reveal an inevitable turning point for your story in Act 2; possibly more than one.

When used as **revelation**, backstory surprises the audience or explains why characters are acting in a certain way. If it means your central character will behave differently now or it forces your readers to re-evaluate their impression of her, then it's working.

This part of a character's backstory is invaluable but use it with care. It can't come out of the blue. Neither should you reveal it too easily, as explained above.

The power of small moments

Never underestimate those small moments when a character thinks she is unobserved or alone. How she behaves may not alter plot but it will reveal how she really feels and this will help the audience to bond. If your teen has a private sketchbook, it could be full of gruesome drawings, for example, where she expresses her negative emotions or idealised images of her dead parents and the family they were.

> TIP: Don't use everything from the backstory that you created for any of your character's storylines. Most of the work you do will lie happily –- or unhappily, muttering small expletives, under the surface or behind the story and need never to be revealed. It's the weight of the iceberg under the surface that makes the crest sharp and shiny.

Act 3: Resolution & Redemption

On to Act 3, but first, go and hug your partner/ cat/ neighbour if they don't object. Do a little joyful dance to your favourite music as loud as you dare and treat yourself to a cup of whatever you fancy most. You might find yourself jotting down notes of things you want to happen in Act 3. You might also need to step away and do something totally different and give your mind a complete break.

There is work yet, but the end of your first draft is in sight.

Having recognised her flaws, your central character is now able to rise and overcome internal tension and story conflict. She finds new strengths, sufficient to defeat the odds still stacked against her. If she trusted someone she shouldn't have or thought the forces of antagonism were less strong, now she knows the truth and there is no internal conflict to distract her from her goal.

You are untangling all the knots you knowingly wove into Acts 1 and 2.

Single-minded and focussed

Your central character now approaches her goal single-mindedly. Time speeds up and it is also running out. The antagonist is now even more determined to defeat or destroy her, one way or another.

Recognition of what she needs to do to end this story should come just in time. Having faced her demons, she will succeed but it won't be easy. There's all of Act 3 to go. There should still be a very real possibility she may not ultimately succeed. This is crucial for suspense. Nobody wants to feel the ending is a foregone conclusion. The difference now is that your central character is focussed in such a way that we know it *is* possible.

We're also more heavily invested because we've seen her go through hell and back and we want her to succeed more than ever.

Redemption and reward

Whether she succeeds or fails, your central character is now redeemed by her actions. Rewarded, she returns to her world with some gift. This gift will differ depending on your story; it could be peace, it could be restoration of the water supply, a magical sword or bringing home some knowledge that is needed.

But it is clear that nothing will ever be the same.

Ideally, it should be better.

So, in Act 3:

- The problem, that is the central dramatic question you posed at the end of Act 1, is resolved.
- As are any other dramatic questions and subplots (see **Subplots** below) you have raised in the course of telling your story.
- Your central character succeeds/ fails/ opts out of her quest/ goal. In this process…
- She becomes a better person, redeemed in some way by her struggle or quest.
- She may bring a reward back to her original world. Depending on your story, this could be knowledge or magic or power. It could be someone she has rescued, access to medicine, water, music or a platinum golf club.
- The big finish/ climax. This leaves us buzzing. (Or arguing, crying, laughing; so long as we are moved!)

Subplots

These can be defined as *additional characters and activity that are in some way germane to the overall story*. In other words, while subplots are generally not essential to your main story, they can:

- Offer additional information about central events,
- Explain or illuminate factors that affect your main story line and
- Feed into your central character's motivations.

For these reasons, subplots often have a theme that is similar to that of your main story or they may reflect upon your core theme by contrasting with the main storyline. For example, let's say your main storyline is the story of a young child discovering she's adopted. After a quarrel with her sister, she runs away to find her birth mother. Desperately worried, her family is trying to find her. So the theme may be about Family Love.

One of your subplots could be about her parents being forced to sell their home.

Depending on how unscrupulous the buyer is, this subplot about greed could shine a light on the theme of love that drives the prime storyline. Maybe the parents sell the family home to have the money to finance their search, or they miss a deadline to object to a compulsory purchase order because finding their child is more important.

Subplot structure

In structure, subplots should have a starting point, pivotal moment of change and end result, but they generally have fewer plot points. Even so, be careful how you thread them through your script. If a subplot peaks too soon or concludes half way through the script, it can make your main plot look anti-climatic.

They rarely contain plot pillars, unless the story information contained in that scene/ sequence is also a key moment in your main plotline. For example, when the two stories collide or overlap and the subplot impacts on your main story.

Let's say one of your subplots involves a car crash, caused by drink/ anger or something else. How might this event effect your central character's motivation and her storyline? If the scene happens after she has fought with the driver, this leads the story in one direction. If the crash involves someone she knows, this could cause a different set of complications. If she witnesses it, if she's in the car, if the car crashes into her, if it causes the death of a detective who was going to give her answers, etc.

Each option will alter the plot and outcome of your story.

In other words, *where* this event happens in your screenplay will have an impact on your main character's motivation and her storyline.

Subplots take up less screen time. They may even be there for light relief.

(Every script can benefit from humour.) Very occasionally, a secondary plot will actually feel like the main story for the readers because of its emotional heft, for example, the love story in *Witness*.

Even a subplot that is there purely for light relief at the start of your script may become crucial and relevant at a later stage.

> TIP: Make a firm decision about what your main story is and what is secondary. Don't get mixed up. Otherwise issues affecting your central dramatic question/ dilemma may be left out or understated, while secondary concerns suddenly get too much screen time. Colour-coding scenes for each storyline can help.

Exercises

1. Outlining Act 2 & 3.

- List your key events and moments, the key plot points you want to use in Act 2. Work out the order that they need to fall in and move them around until it feels right. Does the tension rise from one to the next?
- Now do the same for Act 3.

At this point, you are looking to see if the story works; if it builds from the start of Act 2 onwards to a conclusion. You're roughly plotting the basic structure of your main story. Some parts will fit easily together, others may be slightly interchangeable at the moment and may depend on how your character reacts or develops through the story.

- Once you feel you have the order working, type up your outline for each act and print them out. Take them with you wherever you go in case you get a few minutes to jot down ideas for one moment or another along the outline.

2. Brainstorm the 'in-between' bits

Give yourself ten minutes to brainstorm what might happen in advance of and leading up to each plot point to make it effective. There are two parts to this:

- The practical element: what do we, as reader, need to know for your plot point to work?
- What is the best (or most creative/ unusual) way for us to discover this?

What is the most interesting or speedy way to reach each of these key plot points? See what your imagination throws up. Don't reject anything yet.

Then put it aside and work on the next one.

3. Subplot storylines

As with (1) above, list all your plot points in order for each of the subplots you intend to weave into your main story. Some will be more character-based, others will have plot-based arcs. The latter tend to be easier! Test each subplot storyline on its own by the same criteria:

- Does the story build?
- Is it credible?
- Do we care?
- How does it impact upon the main storyline? Are its plot pillars and turning points at similar points?
- Does it last the length of the script?
- Does it end too soon?
- How does it impact on your central character's motivation?

4. Bringing it all together

Once you are happy with the structure of your individual storylines, you can start weaving your subplots through your main storyline. It helps to colour-code the different storylines by using coloured card or marking the corner of each card with coloured pens – one for each storyline. Several may belong to several storylines, where the stories overlap.

Clear a table, floor or a wall, turn off the phone and spread out one act at a time. Move the subplot scenes around within the main storyline of each act until they start to feel right.

Overlaps

You may find a timeline that seemed perfect in the individual storyline doesn't sit well with the timeline of another storyline. If, for example, much of one of your subplots happens within 24 hours but your main storyline lasts for a weekend; if a subplot needs several days or weeks to come to a conclusion but most of the action in your main storyline happens in a tighter space of time.

In that case you may need to alter the moment at which we come into your subplot, rather than stretch or tighten your main storyline.

In other cases, the chronology of one story will clash with another because certain conditions need to be in place for certain plot points (that you need in that storyline) to happen.

5. Experiment

Try your subplot points in different places within your main storyline. Look at the impact each one has on the momentum of the screenplay if placed in a different position. Outlining often suggests scenes you need and scenes you can cut. You may find you can blend plot points – for example, a romantic encounter you need for Subplot A might happen in the same nightclub that your central character is arriving into for a key scene so you can merge the scenes.

So look at the impact of subplot plot points and scenes:

- on the plot of the main storyline.
- on audience perceptions and emotional well-being;
- on your main character;
- on the structure of the story as a whole.

Do they contribute or distract from your main storyline?
Would they contribute more at a different point in the script?

What needs to have happened by this point for a particular sequence to work?

For example, if you place a key scene from Subplot A after or before a key scene in the main storyline, how would that change the flow of the story?

This is why you need space to spread the story out! You're creating a complex world.

10: Beyond the Three Act

"Of course a film should have a beginning, a middle and an end. But not necessarily in that order."

– Jean-Luc Godard

You can smother a story with formula, often from fear or lack of confidence. I did it myself in the early days with one particular script. Because the structure and plotting of the story became so important, every time I fiddled with it, the story went in a different direction. I had a great start, a wonderful ending, but I could never get it to work all the way through! More worryingly, I wasn't sure what it was I was trying to say.

In the end, after months of work, I had to step away.

So before you fall into that particular abyss, remind yourself that *you are the storyteller*. The three-act formula is a useful and well tested blueprint. It won't suit every story. Learn the demands of structure and then trust your own judgement as to the best way to tell your story.

There is a danger that if you try too hard to fit your story into a formula, you end up asking questions that will produce answers that fit the formula. Especially when you're feeling blocked or lost or overwhelmed.

This can make your story predictable.

What you need to be doing instead is asking questions to see what answers come up. Being this creative, rather than blindly following a set of rules and slotting your script in, may drive you mildly demented. Occasionally you will pull back and panic but your script will be stronger in the end.

And you can do it.

So now you know what the three-act formula is and what it offers, what are the disadvantages of which you might need to be aware.

Cause and effect

In the three-act formula, *story* is more important than *texture*. Nothing exists in your script except for the impact it will have on someone else in your story. As such, the story tends to be linear, constantly moving forward and events are transparent. They exist to show how your central character is changing or to force her to change. They're not arbitrary or open to various interpretations.

This does not mean they need to be obvious or blatantly explained, but it does mean that the reader and audience understand their significance either at the time they happen or later in the story, even if your central character doesn't. Yet. So the end of your story happens as a consequence of everything that's happened before.

This doesn't mean you have to abandon structure to write a thought-provoking script. Just because it's linear does not mean everything happens in an obvious order, but chaos is confusing. If you write a script with no structure at all, your film could become a collection of random interesting (or not) moments. A series of events that are barely connected may intrigue a reader or audience but a whole film structured this way may prove too erratic to give deep emotional satisfaction for the general public.

Morality

Everything in your three-act script works towards your central character recognising her weakness or need. She reaches into herself, overcomes her 'fatal flaw' and finds her inner strength *just in time* to overcome injustice or succeed in her goal. In doing so, she achieves personal redemption and regains self respect.

Good wins out over evil and we celebrate.

It is unrealistic, but then again, you're telling a story. A film with ambiguous characters and an ambiguous message may not satisfy a large audience.

This morality can feel restrictive when you're writing your story. You can't (and shouldn't) force a Doberman into a rabbit hutch and many great films come from breaking away. For example, *Psycho* (written by Joseph Stefano) and *Chinatown*. The flaws and disconnect between this moral form of storytelling and your own idea may be apparent but before you give up on it, see if you can subvert it to suit your story's needs.

If you don't like 'happy' or tidy endings, for example, you can always add a coda – that is, a little sequence of scenes, possibly in voiceover, that happen after the film has officially ended, possibly over (or after) the credits. These can reveal that everything may not be as perfect as it seems.

In a rom-com, for example, the happy-ever-after ending might then have a coda where we hear them beginning to disagree or bicker. In a thriller, it may be that someone we thought was no longer a threat wakes up or makes a phone call.

Practical advantage

From a practical point of view, the advantage of using the three-act formula is that if used well and melded with your imagination, it should make it easier for you to finish your script and to know that your story works as a film. It breaks your script up into manageable units and tells you the key ingredients that you need.

If events in your story lack interest, excitement, humour, logic or relevance; if they happen in an order that fails to create suspense, surprise, anticipation, curiosity or a clear resolution, then your structure is weak and it can be useful to dip back into formula and see what tools are there that might help.

The three-act formula is far from the only one out there, but all of the formulas overlap on the essentials. I would argue that many other formulas are simply different ways of parcelling out the parts that the three-act formula or any well-crafted story generally contains or of more carefully defining smaller particles of story.

Alternative structures

The Hero's Journey (See Appendix C)

I love the language of the Hero's Journey far more than the technical nature of the three-act structure, but the two formulas mirror and complement each other. Devised by Joseph Campbell in his work, *A Man With a Thousand Faces*, it is drawn from his detailed comparative study of myths, legends, folk tales, fairytales and stories that belonged to indigenous communities as a way to understand what were the common elements that we all look for in a satisfying or long-lasting story.

He extracted the key elements they shared and the archetypes, his argument being that this has been a way of telling successful and satisfying stories for millennia, so these were the keys to telling a good story now. Christopher Vogler explains it far better than I can in his book, *The Writer's Journey – Mythic Structure for Storytellers and Screenwriters*.

Four-Act Formula

This works very well for TV since it is designed around the idea that every ad break, 14-15 minutes into a one-hour show, will have to have some cliff-hanger or hook to bring the audience back.

Effectively, since there are three breaks, these could also be said to match Turning Point 1, Mid Point and Turning Point 2, but with a hook at the end to pull us into the next episode.

Five-Act Formula

There were no constraints of time, place or space in the Jacobean and Elizabethan era. Within the five-act structure, there were subplots galore and you could cut back and forth. The purpose of the play was to capture the true energy of life in a space representing the entire world.

Act 1: You introduce the key situation or problem.

Act 2: Now you complicate it, as much as you can.

Act 3: And even more. The situation now becomes intensely complicated.

Act 4: No matter what strategy anyone tries to solve the problem will fail.

Act 5: Finally, failure is dramatically overcome by some action that leads the story to conclude.

The three-act is a model of control. It runs on rails and that suits the industry that is Hollywood. From any point you can see where you've come from and where you're heading. Arguably, in the five act you can get lost in the middle and be utterly immersed with no sight of land, which has a power of its own and arguably might be more suitable for long films.

A final word

Don't let all the dos and don'ts of structural formulas or their expectations faze you. Structure can always be fixed whereas passionate storytelling, having an individual voice, creating genuine characters that intrigue us and scenes that fizzle and spark – these can only come from you.

Granted, it is sometimes a painful rewrite when there are structural issues, but you will know you are working from a strong base. If you want to see the three-act formula in action, the clearest place to see it at work is either in comedies or kids' films.

11: Rules of Thumb

"There is only one plot – things are not what they seem."

– Jim Thompson

Rule 1

The first character we meet should be your central character. Exceptions are stories in which you open with a world that is more interesting or that will ultimately be put under threat.

For example, in *Witness* the film opens in the Amish community while in *One Flew Over the Cuckoo's Nest*, we watch a car travelling to the asylum and then we're in the asylum, because that is the world McMurphy is going to try and change. (Although, technically, since McMurphy is in that car, you could say he is the first character we 'see'!)

Rule 2

Ninety per cent of scenes in your script should feature or affect your main character. If your central character disappears for a huge part of the story, whose story are we really following?

Rule 3

The main character's actions drive the story forward. (See Chapter 4.) If another character is taking up more space than your central character or is causing most of the change in your story, should she be your central character instead? Is your central character too passive or is this a multi-protagonist story?

Rule 4

Most films can only sustain four to six main characters. That is presuming you want to create characters with depth. When you stretch this rule, for example with the film *Slacker* (written by Richard Linklater) which has a large ensemble cast, you are clearly trying something different.

In that case, you will need to draw your audience in with some other aspect of the screenplay such as the world, the quirkiness of the characters or the way you explore the theme. In the case of *Slacker*, we go on a picaresque journey through time; incidents and scenarios are interesting and quirky but we only get to know the characters superficially as we travel through the day on campus.

Rule 5

The dramatic question/ problem you raise at the end of Act 1 must be resolved in Act 3.

Rule 6

The only rule to break at your peril is this one: **There must be something compelling on screen all the time.** It might be an interesting character, magical or witty dialogue, an unusual or intriguing set-up/ location/ image/ event. It could be the tension building or it could be time out with a slow-moving but deeply emotional scene, but you must keep us engaged.

You don't want anyone to be able to step back from your story, as readers or viewers.

12: Powerful Writing: The Individual Scene

"I love writing, but hate starting. The page is awfully white and it says, 'You may have fooled some of the people some of the time but those days are over, Giftless. I'm not your agent and I'm not your mommy: I'm a white piece of paper. You wanna dance with me?' and I really, really don't. I'll go peaceable-like."

— Aaron Sorkin

The individual scene is the basic unit of your screenplay but it comes in all sizes and shapes. A scene may be one line long or run for several pages. It may be mostly dialogue, mostly action or a mixture of both. Whatever its style or tone – whether it is dramatic, fragmented, slow-moving, every scene has to have a reason to be in your script. It is whatever you need at that point in your story.

Some will flow easily as you write; others will feel like dredging mud. But, right now, the important thing is to get them written and move the story on.

As we established in Chapter 6, you could be talking any number of scenes from one hundred and sixty to two hundred and twenty. So, before we dive in, some theory to move you in the right direction.

1. Character

Every scene can tell us something about character.

It may introduce a new character or reveal something interesting about a relationship or a character trait. A reaction, even understated or ignored, can tell us a lot. For example, something a character does could reveal her attitude to another character, make us more curious or suspicious about her, or more understanding.

Maybe in the course of a scene we witness behaviour of which she's totally unaware but which gives us a clue to her backstory. It might not even be noticed by anyone in the scene.

You know your characters. This does not mean they know themselves. If you were to ask five people to describe a mutual acquaintance, each will most likely use different words or focus on different traits.

Through behaviour (description and action) and dialogue, you bring your characters to life. Don't waste the opportunity to, however subliminally, allow us to discover more about them by how they act in a given situation.

2. Story

Every scene has a duty to move your story forward.

This could be by revealing some crucial information or planting a clue, the value of which will only be understood later. It could be by introducing a critical new character. It may be that something happens in the scene that forces your central character to act and changes what happens next. It might be the revelation of a tiny bit of information that leads to the next scene happening in a certain way or in a particular place and having a different outcome to the one your characters expect.

3. Entertainment

To entertain your readers and eventual viewers.

You are in control of how your readers feel. Every scene has the capacity to make us cry, laugh, turn the page greedily or be glued to the screen when your script is filmed. You decide how you want us to feel at the start and end of every scene. Once you have achieved this, you move on.

~ ~ ~

Every single scene should manage to incorporate at least two of these functions. Why? Because if a scene addresses two or more, it will be a stronger, richer scene, working harder to tell your story.

Having worked out what you need to achieve through your step outline, you may find yourself merging scenes so that they are stronger or deleting them because they can be cut without affecting the story or because their role in the story is too similar to other scenes.

Layers of story

Most scenes can be said to have two layers: what the scene is obviously about and what it is about beneath the surface.

The surface layer

The most obvious in terms of structure, this layer describes the main purpose of the scene. It tends to be action or conflict-oriented, most obviously driving the story forward but it can also be more superficial or sensational.

Essentially, this layer reveals information we need. What this information is depends on the position of the scene within your story. It could be about a relationship, about the antagonist, a revelation that changes everything, if only slightly, or you may be planting a clue that will make sense further on.

Let's go back to the earlier scenario of Alice, the best friend who betrays your central character. If you write a scene in which your central character is looking for keys in Alice's backpack and finds a cheque addressed to her from the antagonist, that would be the surface layer of your scene. It is crucial plot information.

The sub-surface layer

This is at least as important as the surface layer. Generally to do with character and relationships, it tends to be less overt because it is the layer that reveals something we need to know emotionally.

As such, it tends to be directed at helping us bond *with character* or add depth to the emotional or relationship aspect of the scene and your story. It can be interior action, quite subtle or subliminal. For example, in the sub-surface layer of a scene we might realise one character feels uncomfortable in another person's company, in this particular setting or talking about a certain subject. We can see that she is distracted or frustrated or angry but we don't know why yet.

In the scenario used to demonstrate the surface layer, above, what if your central character was about to propose that Alice move in with her, or if she suspected that Alice was getting tired or her or was having an affair. Maybe your central character thinks she's pregnant and doesn't know how to deal with it yet? Maybe she has lied about sleeping with her ex-husband so she comes to the scene full of guilt. Any of these elements could happily co-exist in the scene in which she discovers Alice's betrayal.

~ ~ ~

Getting in deeper to the actual writing of the scene, there are three golden rules to always keep in mind:

Three Golden Rules

1. Show don't tell

You write what you hope we will see on the screen. If it isn't on the screen, we can't know it so if a character *feels* something, we need to *see* how it affects her within the scene you've written. You need to find a way to make it visible.

Whether your character is trying to hide how she feels, whether this feeling is taking her by surprise or she's happy to own it will affect her behaviour in a scene.

I've had students say that they write what a character feels in direction so that the actor will know what to emote. It is more professional and makes for a more interesting screenplay if you show how your character feels through her behaviour or if it comes out through the words she speaks because of how she feels when put under pressure.

Each decision you make for your character will change how she acts within that scene. This behaviour, whether it's action or reaction, large or small, extremely subtle or dramatic, must be in the scene for us to understand.

2. Less is more

Audiences are intelligent. It may be more powerful to show an understated reaction or to cut out that speech that *explains* everything. Readers will get it, without you spelling out what a character feels or thinks and/ or without giving us her whole speech.

If there is a lot of dialogue but it isn't actually changing the mood, moving the story on or telling us a whole heap more about character, could you replace some of it with action or cut away to your next scene, leaving us wanting more?

For example, it might be enough to see a character arguing behind the glass window of the gym and storming out than for us to hear every word of the row, especially if we already know what the row is about? If you have a character making a long political speech, maybe cut away to someone reacting to what he said and cover the rest of the speech in this way?

In *On the Waterfront*, Terry has to tell Evie (Eve Marie Saint) about his role in her brother's death. It's a crucial and inevitable scene, both for their relationship and the plot – but we already know this information. So the scene happens in the distance. It's a short scene in which we hear not one word but we see her reaction and we know what has happened.

3. Begin late, leave early

Following on from the previous rule, how much of the argument do we really need to hear? What if all we see is her reaction as she climbs into her car or walks into a stranger outside the gym because she's so angry/ upset/ scared?

Often, you will need to write an argument out in detail before you work out what parts of it you need to include or to find lines that resonate powerfully. These may be all you ever put in the script from that row. Don't worry about this. It's a crucial stage sometimes – and I often do it myself. It's a way of stepping into a situation, experiencing the moment with your characters as it happens. If you cut it out later or cut the dialogue back, the rest is under the surface like subtext, making the scene stronger.

Of course, to end a scene once the point is made, you need to know why you are writing that scene and how you want your readers and eventual audience to feel at the end of it. Once you've achieved that, you get out and move on.

So where to begin?

Attitude

Every character enters a scene with history. They have an opinion or attitude towards the other person or people in the scene, towards themselves, towards the reason for this meeting or encounter if there is one, expectation of how the day/ evening/ meeting will pan out, etc.

Your central character is meeting her father for lunch to find out something about her birth mother. A simple scenario but, depending on the story you are weaving, it could be an immensely important scene. Look for a moment at the range of emotions, attitudes, opinions each of these two people could have before the meeting, during and after, depending on how it goes.

In another scenario, your central character is meeting a former colleague who may be working for the antagonist. If the employee blames her for his dismissal, he may arrive at the scene still holding a grudge or thinking he might be getting his job back. Is he willing to blackmail her to get his job back? Whichever one you decide to use creates one level of tension before the scene even begins. On the other side, if your central character is unaware of the circumstances of his dismissal, if she likes him or thinks he likes her, if they had an affair, if she doesn't actually remember him as an individual, all of these will change how the scene runs.

For drama you need conflict

Once you know what your characters want from a scene, part of the joy as a screenwriter is making it as difficult for your character as possible so that you get the outcome you want from the scene. Something, however small, has changed.

Look at the opening of the breakfast scene in *As Good As It Gets*. It starts upbeat. Carol is looking forward with happiness to her date that evening. We know her child is ill but even this is revealed by her talking about him in an amazed and upbeat fashion – he promised not to get ill on her date. Then Udall arrives.

By the end of the scene, he has said something without thinking, something logical and painfully true that has whipped the floor out from under her. He has stated that her son is probably going to die sooner than most. She forces him to acknowledge this, by warning him that if he ever mentions her son again, he'll never be able to eat at that restaurant again. She reminds him that he is powerless here.

She hits him where she knows it will hurt, not by saying she won't talk to him again because that wouldn't matter to him at this point. Their relationship has changed. Her good mood is gone. And he has been made to acknowledge that he said something inappropriate and without thinking that hurt someone he needs badly.

Let's say you have a character returning home to her partner at the end of a day. What might influence how she acts coming into this scene and how she reacts to whatever you have decided will happen in this scene?

- How happy she feels in this relationship.
- How well her day has gone.
- Whether she has news she wants to share or news that she wants to hide.
- Whether she has delayed coming home or was delayed by someone who told her something she didn't want to hear.
- If she is no longer in love.
- If she's afraid of her partner, if she's even aware that she is or in denial.
- If she feels haunted by something.
- f she has waited all day for this moment.
- If she's concerned about her partner's health, mental or physical.
- If she's worried about the bills she hasn't paid.

The point is that whatever you choose, it will have an impact on how the scene will play.

Questions to ask:

What is your story or surface level goal for this scene?

Knowing what your goal is for a scene will help you choose the elements you need to make it work. For example, you want Character A to admit (reluctantly/ defiantly/ ecstatically?) that she has lost her job. Despite the fact that this is what will happen in your scene, let's say your character enters it determined to keep up the charade of her 'good' job. Why might she do this? Is she proud, afraid of something or doesn't want to disappoint her partner? Maybe this is the third job she's lost in a month?

What can you do to bring her to the point of admitting that she has lost her job?

What is the sub-surface or emotional goal of the scene?

Continuing with the scenario above, depending on Character A's attitude going into the scene (her attitude to self, partner, job, the world), will she say something that accidentally reveals a clue to the truth that her partner leaps upon? Will she blurt out her news in anger because of something her partner says or assumes that makes her feels trapped? Does she want an emotional reaction and therefore throws the news at her partner to see what will happen? Does her partner goad or push her in some way so that she snaps? Or is she suddenly too tired to lie anymore?

How do you want us to feel when the scene ends?

Staying with character, you need to know how each of your characters in the scene handle this news. This will tell us a huge amount almost subliminally about their relationship, about the characters themselves, their attitudes, personalities, how they feel about their lives and so on.

- Why does she feel she has to lie, for example?
- Will the scene be dramatic, funny, sad?
- How do you want us to feel when it ends?

Once we feel that way and you have achieved your goals in terms of story and character, you leave that scene and move on.

Finding predicament

Scenes that have no real predicament do not work. They are scenes in which nothing changes. Even if the dialogue is bouncing off the page, if the scene is merely establishing the arrival of your character outside the hotel in which a meeting is to be held, it can usually be cut without altering the story.

This isn't to say that that something major has to happen in each scene. It doesn't. But the story has to move on, relationships have to develop, things have to be revealed about character or story, even if they seem unimportant at the time.

> TIP: Something has to be at stake in the scene. It doesn't have to be huge and it might not be acknowledged by the players in the scene, but there has to be something. It might be how one character is thought of by the other person, the loss of her good mood, that she doesn't get something she needs or can't make herself understood.

13: Dialogue and Character

"A few words can have underneath them a whole world. 90% of writing isn't in the words you read, it's what's underneath them, holding them up."

– Stephen Cleary

Conventional film wisdom tells us that that dialogue is less important than image. But here's the thing: when your dialogue feels authentic, your characters feel real. It's that simple. Good dialogue shows you have an ear for the way people speak. This implies that you understand human nature and that means you can write credible characters. It doesn't slow story down, or worse, stop it dead.

Getting to that point isn't automatic for all writers but it can be learnt. And it's worth doing well.

You can recognise a stage adaptation instantly in a film script. Often not because of the limited number of locations, lack of visual scope or the size of the cast but because it's too dialogue-heavy or the dialogue is too theatrical.

I'm writing this as a writer who loves dialogue. And there are exceptions.

Everyone can think of at least one film as memorable for its dialogue as its plot. In *The Maltese Falcon*, dialogue is as much a dramatic player in its own right as any of the characters are. Other exceptions are character-driven films such as *The Lady in the Van* (written by Alan Bennett) or *Who's Afraid of Virginia Woolf?* (screenplay by Ernest Lehman, based on Edward Albee's stage play).

However, even in plot-driven scripts, where there is noticeably less dialogue, it is crucial to make every word count.

So how do you use dialogue to help you tell your story? In many ways, the functions dialogue can fulfil echo those of the individual scene:

Character

The way we speak

The speed at which we speak, how we vocalise, pronounce and articulate, all these carry with them indications of background, age, upbringing, occupation, personality, emotional state and attitudes.

The words we use

The words a character uses in any situation are determined by how she feels about herself, about the person she is talking to, about the issue, the day, this meeting, this place, whether she is hiding or trying to hide something and so on. Think about it. How any of your characters talk in a scene could vary depending on whether she likes the person she is talking to, if she *really* likes them, if she finds them creepy, amusing or terrifying. Or how good she is at disguising how she feels. It's very simple, really. If she has no choice but to be in a certain scene, your character will speak differently than if she wants to be there.

The words we choose

Dialogue can deceive, of course and this can be a useful character trait. If a character affects different accents depending on the company she is in, for example.

Plot

What a character says in a scene helps define the plot because it depends on her role in your story. Whether your character reveals information or keeps a secret, for example; which in turn might depend on who she's talking to, how badly they want the information and how high the stakes are for your character.

Entertainment

You can use dialogue to relieve tension, through humour; to put us at ease.

Useful tips for writing good dialogue

1. Characters: secrets and lies

Know what your characters want to say or to avoid saying before they enter a scene. What any character says in a scene can reveal her emotional state, a personality quirk or trait, conflict between characters, within her and within the story. Don't waste those lines!

2. Motivation

Know why your characters are here, in this scene, now.

- Know how they feel about being there.
- Know how they feel about the subject in hand.
- Know what they want from this scene
- What is each character's relationship with other players in the scene; is it known or unknown?

Then, return to the reader and ask yourself:

- How or what do you want us to feel at the end of this scene?

3. Individual voices

Each character should have her own voice throughout the script. While this is something you probably consciously do when you start a script – I know, for me, the voices are in my head and I often find myself talking their lines as I type! – but once you get deep into plotting or the complexity of the story takes over, sometimes the voices can begin to blur and sound similar.

An early work of mine got a reader's comment along the lines of, 'Every character is you'. Trust me, that is NOT what you want to hear! You should be able to cover the names and still tell who is speaking at any time.

It's not about verbal tics or dialect, jargon or key phrases/ words that they use. It's about the rhythm, the tone, the attitude, the history their voices carry. With the film, *In Bruges* (written by Martin McDonagh) the older, mentor criminal Ken (Brendan Gleeson) always sounds rather elegant in his use of language while his friend Ray (Colin Farrell) sounds like a sulky teenager.

Having said all this, don't worry if this isn't happening yet or doesn't happen in every scene. You can fix it in the next draft. The most important thing right now is to get the dialogue down on the page, but it helps to have an awareness of what you want to achieve. Later, you can take troublesome scenes with you to a cafe, reward yourself with your favourite drink and make your characters talk about themselves.

Alternatively, invite a bunch of friends around and ask them to read the scenes aloud so you can hear your characters speak.

4. Establishing character

Don't let one slice of dialogue skew your characters off track.

As soon as a character speaks, you establish her for us. We learn something about her personality, opinions and attitudes by what she says or doesn't say. Be careful of (accidentally) establishing an attitude or dialogue trait in a scene that you hadn't intended to be part of your character throughout the script.

Dialogue that may be fun to write in one scene could cause problems for you later. I've fallen down this particular pothole myself. The problem arises when – not wanting to lose that segment – you find yourself trying to weave in similar attitude/ speech patterns into that character's other scenes throughout the script.

For example, a character who becomes hilariously witty in one scene for no reason other than that the words came to you. Do you make a point of showing how odd this is for this character? (She gets teased about her 'performance', it's referred to afterwards as 'that time when you…' or there's a sideways comment about wanting 'whatever she's on'. There are many ways.) Or do you try to make her wittier throughout the script?

The trick is to know why you're doing this. Adjusting a character's personality and behaviour to fit with a line or segment of dialogue in a scene can be problematic for the story as a whole. If the changed behaviour is inappropriate to a scene or jars with the story, it could damage your story or the credibility of your characterisation.

For example, a quirky/ sarcastic remark or style of speaking might brighten the dialogue in one scene but if it doesn't fit a character who's quite shy, changing her behaviour and dialogue elsewhere to match may be to the detriment of your story.

However, it is also possible that you have accidentally stumbled on a trait that will actively enrich your character, story, tone, etc. If your shy character, for example, becomes quirky or sarcastic when she's nervous or when she's really comfortable, that could be interesting to use.

Following on from this…

5. Know what your characters are thinking

Dialogue conveys a character's attitude towards other characters. If it is used only to dish out information or tells us exactly what we need to know, it soon becomes lifeless or artificial. (This is known as 'on the nose' dialogue, where information is given far too literally. See **Dialogue Danger Zones** below.)

The simplest response can convey a character's attitude towards herself. What she says and the words she chooses to say it with, may depend on how comfortable she is:

- Saying what she is saying or needs to say;
- About what she is *able* to say in this situation;
- In the company she is in.

6. Action speaks louder than words

In real life, it can be impossible to express yourself during an argument, when feeling emotional, exhausted or when you've just heard disturbing news, let alone to find the right words. Don't be afraid to use silence or action in your script. A shrug might be more effective than a verbal response. If your characters are always able to respond with the right words, it can feel unreal or contrived.

Dialogue is better at expressing thoughts than feelings or emotions.

It might be more effective emphasising a character's difficulty in expressing herself. Perhaps, rather than answering a question directly, she changes the subject, answers a different question, doesn't respond at all?

Is there's an action or gesture that would express how she feels more accurately and with greater impact, for example? Rubbing her eyes, shifting in the seat, a sigh might be more revealing of boredom than a line of dialogue saying how bored she is.

7. Style of dialogue

Naturalistic

This is the most popular form of film dialogue. It feels real because it sounds like everyday speech and so tends not to not draw attention to itself. This allows us to focus on the information it reveals.

While realistic, using naturalistic dialogue is no excuse to ramble. Screenplay dialogue is written for the ear, not the eye. Your script is there to entertain and the dialogue needs to be wittier, sharper, more interesting than normal. Don't clutter scenes with social chatter, unless you have an important point to make. In any script, words and sentences are meticulously selected, even if the end result feels as natural as everyday speech.

Unless you conspicuously want to emphasise an important aspect of the story or to distance us from a character for some reason, naturalistic dialogue is usually the best choice but there are alternatives.

Theatrical

A stylised use of words, theatrical dialogue calls attention to itself and loves the limelight. Take this dialogue from Sam Spade (Humphrey Bogart) in *The Maltese Falcon*: "*You won't need much of anybody's help. You're good. It's chiefly your eyes, I think, and that throb you get in your voice when you say things like, 'Be generous, Mr. Spade.'*"

<u>Minimalistic</u>

Unnaturally terse, even staccato, minimalistic dialogue allows no time for niceties or feelings. It emphasises and intentionally reinforces the gulf between character and ordinary people. For example, Arnold Schwarznegger in *Terminator 2* (written by James Cameron and William Wisher) is consciously abrupt, with lines like: "*I'm sorry, John. I'm sorry,*" "*I must go away*" and "*It has to end here*".

8. Dialogue is two-sided: Action/ reaction

You're not looking for the easiest response but the one that contains the most information on character, plot and the world of your film. Play with your readers; subvert their expectations. How do they expect your character to react?

Instead of answering a question, what if she misunderstood, misheard, took offence, didn't respond, changed the subject, drew someone else into the conversation, walked away or laughed?

Dialogue Danger Zones

On the nose

This is dialogue that says exactly what it means and gives information directly and literally to your reader that the writer believes they need to know. Once you look for it, you will see it everywhere. One TV series I'm currently dipping into does it in such a way it keeps driving me from the room! So avoid it. Never state the obvious. There is always a different way to let us know something we need to know.

There is a joke that the only time a character will say *I love you* eventually is in soap. In a screenplay, having created this wonderful world full of characters for us and with limited time to tell your story, there are oodles of more creative ways to say or to show this. By making the person she loves her favourite meal, asking her how she is, telling her a story that will make her happy, doing or saying something that *shows* her feelings. It's faster and it's more effective.

Over the top

This is dialogue that is way bigger than the dialogue you would hear in normal life; where every emotion is extreme and expressed, as in melodrama. Melodramatic dialogue has its place. Just not often in a screenplay, unless it's a character trait or an essential element of the world you've created.

Polemic

Don't preach, unless you can do it subtly. Preaching stops the flow of a story stone dead. A script has to work as entertainment. Otherwise whatever moral you would like to demonstrate is lost.

Repetition

Dialogue can say the same thing in totally different ways. This can be really hard to see until you're re-reading a scene with a bit of distance. It could mean you can cut everything that happens in between or it may mean removing the least original version.

But it can be difficult to spot.

You can say something about being bored at work in an infinite number of ways. For example, having your character complaining about the boss or colleagues, about a project or work in general, about the atmosphere in the workplace, the decor, the attitude of colleagues, how long the day is, pranks staff play because they're unchallenged, excuses she makes to leave the office on jobs that she stretches so that she doesn't have to return and so on.

All could work well but if your goal is to show your character is bored at work, one of these may be plenty.

However, let's say you want to build the scene from a character being loath to admit she finds her job dull to admitting that she hates every moment of it, then you might use a few of them, provided more is revealed each time about how she really feels. How you engineer this may depend on whether she's talking to a colleague, to the owner of the firm or to her partner (and they need the money the job brings in).

The scene could go from pretending she loves her job, "*all the little details, always the same, one after the other…*" to wanting to blow the office up so she never has to return. The point is that the *information* given *under* the dialogue is changing – it's not 'I'm bored' so much as 'I'm fine, okay' which can work its way to, 'I'm not totally fine, okay' and finally to 'I'm catastrophically un-fine'.

Tongue-twisters

A Scottish solider was shot in the shoulder. The idea of putting a line like this into your script might seem ludicrous but lines can be tongue-twisters without being this extreme. Read them aloud if you can and avoid lines that are difficult to read, unless you are doing it deliberately. It's cruel to ask an actor to show emotion if they have to try and not trip up while saying your dialogue.

Speech directions

These appear in parenthesis before dialogue. (See Chapter 16 on **Format**.) Try to avoid having too many; it can make the script look unprofessional if you keep telling us how a character should speak (*happily, slowly, chirpily* etc). Trust the characters you have created and the dialogue you have written. Most of the time it will be perfectly clear how the lines should be interpreted and delivered.

One clear exception is if there are technical reasons you need to direct the actors (or the readers). For example, in a multi-handed scene where a character is addressing different people, then you might use such directions as: *To:- / Cutting in:-/ Over.*

Jargon

Jargon can be useful for establishing character or time and place, but it can date very quickly and can also alienate readers, if it's overdone.

Clichés

'Giving it 110%', 'In a nutshell', 'Game-changer', 'At the end of the day', 'No place like home' and so on. These are stilted, world weary phrases so use them with care and only if appropriate to character. For example, if a certain character uses cliché and it is always embarrassing; maybe this habit is mocked by others.

Alternatively:

1. Think of original replacements; different ways to express old truisms.

2. Use half-clichés where you substitute one of the subjects to comic or other effect.

3. Find more unusual analogies and expressions that have a familiar feel and that seem appropriate.

Dialect

There are two elements to dialect: Speech patterns and vocabulary. Make sure you're familiar with both or you can unintentionally create offensive caricatures.

You may choose to mirror the different sentence construction. For example, take *In The Name Of The Father*. When Gerry's father (Pete Postlethwaite) announces he is off to bring Gerry home from jail in the UK, he says, *I'm away over to London*.

Not, I'm going to London or I'm off to London.

Alternatively, you can opt to highlight a character's accent at the start of the speech and get it out of the way. For example:

<pre>
                    JACK
               (French accent)
         Hello fellow screenwriter.
</pre>

Or

<pre>
                    JACK
              (In a French accent)
         Hello fellow screenwriter.
</pre>

Alternatively you could use well-known foreign phrases or slang within the speech.

<pre>
                    JACK
         Bonjour fellow screenwriter.
</pre>

Two-handers

These are scenes in which two characters talk to each other. Depending on what happens within the scene, two-handers can be uncinematic and slow, if they go on for more than a page and nothing changes by the end of the scene.

What can you do?

- Add extra characters

Don't add extra characters for the sake of it. If, however, the arrival of another character or characters means something dramatic can happen that needs to happen at this point in your story, go for it.

- Dramatise the scene

Is the scene necessary? If so, look at what else might happen at this point, in this scene. Is all the dialogue necessary? A shorter, sharper scene might be more effective. Could it be merged with another scene for more action/ energy? Do you need to add tension? Does anything actually happen in the scene, at least beneath the surface, to justify the scene taking up screen time?

Work out what do you want to have achieved with this scene. Then remove the clutter so the scene achieves this and get on to the next one.

Stress individual words

Underlining or putting occasional words in bold is only advisable if doing so will affect our understanding of that sentence. Don't do it unless:

1. Stressing one word or phrase will change the meaning and our understanding of what said

2. It is necessary to indicate mood, attitude and disposition of speaker. For example, '*How high should I go?*' versus '*How high should I go?*' The first might suggest nervousness; the second could imply that the speaker regards herself as a far better climber than the other climber(s). But behaviour, allied with the sentence, could be just as revealing and remove the need to stress any individual word.

For fun, try emphasising a different word in the following sentence each time you say it, 'I never said you were stupid'. The meaning and inference changes each time.

In the majority of cases, however, you can trust your characters. We will know from everything that has gone before and what they say now whether they are being suspicious, sarcastic or loving. Unless you are setting us up to be shocked or surprised later.

Speech patterns

Good dialogue is jumpy and disconnected. People interrupt, they take offence, they misunderstand (sometimes deliberately), they change the subject, they don't finish sentences.

- Question and answer

Question and declarative sentence followed by question response feels awkward and unreal as do questions to which the response is another question. Try it!

Who are you?

Kitty. Why are you asking?

Because I want to know. Why shouldn't I?

You have no right. Why should you ask me anything?

It's a nice day. Why are you so defensive ?

Or

Who are you?

Why should I tell you?

What are you hiding?

What's it to you?

Now try writing a scene in which every question gets a logical answer:

Who are you?

Miriam.

Why are you here?

I'm waiting for someone.

They are fun to do but they feel seriously unreal and you'll instinctively learn how to avoid them!

- Avoid long speeches.

Long speeches can make readers restless. Screenwriting is, ultimately, a visual medium. We take information in more easily with our eyes than our ears.

So what are your options? Can you cut the speech down? Do you need it all? Can you break it down into shorter segments, keep some of it for later or give some of it to another character as a reaction, maybe a contradictory one? Could some of it be visual or involve action? Could it be voiceover over contradictory visuals?

- Identical speech lengths

If each speech is exactly the same length as the one preceding it, it doesn't look right on the page. Besides, people don't speak that way. Can you cut lines or replace them with behaviour?

Do leave:
Pregnant pauses. Spaces between words. Choked emotions. Hesitation.

Hold back:
Don't say everything.

Be ruthless:
Again, less is more. Come into an argument half way through. Or leave early. See how it feels. Every line you save allows you to write another more interesting one later!

Testing dialogue

- Read it aloud.
- Cover the names and see if you can tell who's speaking.

When I'm sketching out scenes, I never write the names of who's speaking each line on the page. I presume (hope!) that I will know who's speaking when I type the scene into the computer. Each character is different and each will express herself in a different way, using different words. How she reacts will also depend on how she feels today and with this other person.

At least, that's how it's *meant* to be!

Alternatively, get a group together, bribe them with chocolate and get them to read through a couple of scenes so you can hear them. It's amazing how useful it can be.

Exercises

1. Listen to him

Take the sentence: *Listen to him. He's your father.* I want you to write the response.

Your task is to decide who is speaking and who is responding, in what circumstances, where it happens and why. This will inform the response – verbal or physical – that you come up with. It should reveal something about the relationship between the initial speaker and the person who responds. See where it leads…

Try making it into an argument, into a tragic or comic scene; could you even make it turn into a romantic scene?

2. Voices from the book

Open a book at random and lift out a line of dialogue. Make yourself write a conversation between two characters that begins or ends with this line.

Now change the age, gender, circumstance of the speakers and start again. See if you can make this line lead you into a love scene, a scene revealing something and a fight.

3. Into hot (or cold) water

Think of three uncomfortable situations your central character would normally avoid and put her into each of them. Let her (try to) talk her way out of it.

14: Creating Vivid Description

"If it's not on the page, it will never magically appear on the screen."

– Richard E Grant

Unfortunately, visual storytelling is not a matter of adding visuals to the dialogue, of adding a few paragraphs describing the scene or slipping the odd action or two between speeches. Equally, a nice passage of descriptive prose, describing all the elements we can see and hear but in which nothing happens, risks losing most of your readers.

In film, dialogue rarely has the same impact as it does on stage, while a look or fidgeting with a pen, might. Take Christopher Walken as the homicidal sadist Rovert in *The Comfort of Strangers* (written by Harold Pinter based on Ian McEwan's novel.). There's a moment in that film when he merely twitches one eyebrow and your gut instinct is to tell the other characters in the scene to flee. Now!

But of course, in the interests of the story, they don't notice. (See Chapter 6.) We know he's dangerous; the couple he has befriended don't. That is what gives the story its power and makes the gesture so unsettling.

Ten tips for writing effective description for the screen

- Everything should be in the present tense. Essentially, you are describing on the page what we see on screen now. And only that.
- Avoid passive descriptions. For example: He *starts to* walk, *begins to* drink. Your character *walks*, *drinks*. Similarly, use active, punchy verbs. They are far more effective and generally tell us more about a

character's attitude/ personality. For example, *she prowls the room* is stronger than *she walks around the room.*

- Be aware of time passing in your story. Either dramatise it or cut to next scene. Avoid, on pain of a subconscious rebuke from me, *after a while, eventually, finally.* It's too vague. How long do we wait? And what is happening while we wait?

- Be conscious of how long a scene will run on screen. Let's say you write five paragraphs describing the beauty of that poppy field in Chapter 1. If the camera were to cover everything in those paragraphs, it could take several shots. Meanwhile, what is happening to the characters?

- Write in short concise sentences. We don't need literature; we want the story to keep moving. *She wears an elegant red gown* is as effective as *she wears a long dress in red silk with a dramatic slash up to the thigh and pearls around the hem* but takes up less space and leaves you an extra line to play with later.

- Think description through in your head visually. How would it actually look on screen? Then describe what we will see in a way that will emotionally engage us.

- Avoid clutter. Do not add any information that is not essential to that particular moment in time. Save it for when we need to know unless you are planting something, the value of which we will learn later.

- Keep camera angles to a minimum. They pull the reader back out of your story. Only add camera moves if they are a key element in the action of the scene. Even then it is possible to write in a style that suggests the shots of a scene instead.

- When in doubt, leave space. Make the script easy to read.

Character

Character is action. What your characters do on screen tells us what we need to know about their emotional state and how they feel. Think of a character trying to hide her feelings of distaste from another character, her feelings of discomfort, of love, of fear in public and in private. How do you dramatise these scenes so that your readers understand what's happening but, if necessary, the other characters in these scenes don't?

Appearance:

Always give a character's age, at least roughly, when you introduce them to us. Otherwise, only include details if that are relevant. It's more important to give an overall impression than a list of specific details such as hair colour or style, unless this is really important to how we understand and see her.

You might say, "Dresses smartly, regardless of the day" but you wouldn't necessarily describe the style of suit, the colour, the creases in her trousers and her shiny shoes. Ask yourself, *What type of person does she seem to be?* and then show us.

Behaviour/ action:

Ideally, when you introduce a character to us, she is doing something that reveals an aspect of her nature, her attitude to herself or to other characters, or what is worrying her. Someone slamming a coffee cup on the table so hard that the handle breaks off is more memorable than the same person saying, "I am angry" or another character commenting on her mood. Showing a character suppressing – or attempting to suppress – an emotion can be far more powerful on screen and takes skill to write.

Look for ways to show or dramatize a character's emotional state. How a character behaves in a scene adds rhythm and articulates the changing beats of a scene. But also ask yourself, is this description filmable?

Don't worry about revealing how a character feels through their behaviour. Your readers do need to know, but it has to be visible on the page. If you use speech directions, do it sparingly. Try to avoid adjectives and find a physical way to illustrate the same. For example, instead of having *nervously* as a speech direction, you might have:

> *(trying to hide his nervousness)*
> *(swallowing hard*
> *(speaking quickly)*
> *(growing heated)*

Describing action

Put in everything that affects the pacing and dramatic flow of the scene, either as parenthetical instructions under the character's name or as paragraphs of description interspersed with dialogue.

Some practical examples:

> *(Sighing)*

> She pauses to let this sink in.
> He takes a few breaths to steady himself before continuing.
> They walk together in silence, each waiting for the other to speak first

Dialogue is great for expressing thoughts, but behaviour expresses feelings and emotion. For readers, they are far more important, especially when they can't be revealed. Yet.

What to use:

Be careful that the action you describe doesn't distract from the mood and character you're developing. What you choose to describe will also depend on whose point of view you are focusing on in this scene and what you want us to see and know. We don't have to see a reaction from everyone in a scene. Know who is important for us to be aware of and then let us see their reaction.

Describing internal thoughts

Be careful of describing a character's internal thoughts. We can't see what a character is thinking until she responds physically. That response might be as simple as taking a step back, moving away, grimacing, scratching the palm of her hand, playing with keys – but it has to be visual.

Make it visible without drawing more attention or time to something for longer than it is worth.

Beats of action

Break action into 'beats'. That is, put each distinct incident or change of action in a separate paragraph. If she throws a punch and the other character falls to the ground, clutching their nose, this might be enough for one beat and deserve a paragraph of its own. Hit return and, in the next beat, the other character gets to her feet, pulling a screwdriver from her back pocket and so on.

Breaking the action up makes it easier to read but also easier for the reader to work out how long the scene will run in reality. It also makes readers feel they are moving faster. Nobody wants to get bogged down trying to unravel what happens in a long paragraph.

It may also help you to realise what's important to that scene and hone it down so that the scene is tighter and faster still.

Time

If you have a character leaving one scene and arriving at a different location for a later scene, how much time has to pass before they arrive and what happens meanwhile? Let's say your character leaves her workplace and the next scene is in her home, but that journey takes an hour.

You can cut straight to the next scene or use the time for parts of another storyline or involving another character's arc.

Description of scene

Make full use of setting, objects, sound, colour to add layers of meaning to scene and look for conflict, even if it's under the surface. If you are describing a location relevant to a character, think about the type of person she is.

But, as with characters, props must be necessary or have a function. Avoid clutter for the sake of it. It's not necessary to describe everything in a location or setting. If the bookshelves are overflowing with feminist literature, that's a detail that could be important. The position of the window, the number of chairs, a list of all the authors on the shelf might not, while the Scooby Doo rug might.

If you want a character to feel uncomfortable in a scene, how can you re-work or create a location that will highlight this? How much more interesting might it be to show someone having to hide their sorrow at a party in their honour, their favourite niece's party, a book launch? Such a choice might lead to a stronger scene than seeing her at a funeral home, where we expect sorrow.

Music

I'm often asked about whether it's a good idea to include specific music in a script. It depends. You might say, 'Michael Jackson's *Thriller* plays off screen'. If this song is utterly crucial to the scene or story because of the theme/ setting/ events happening in that scene, that's one issue. It may be possible to purchase the rights to use the music in that scene, if the cost can be justified by the script.

If, on the other hand, you're suggesting the tone or style of the music you feel the script needs, that's different and say so. This lets the reader know that if *Thriller* can't be used, something similar will work in its place. For example, you might specify *1980s disco-rock such as Jackson's Thriller.*

Description danger zones

Set-up scenes

Pure set-up scenes are often the first to be cut by a producer or director, or by the writer working on a later draft. You may not need a scene in which a character arrives outside a location in which there is to be a meeting. It might be better to cut straight to the meeting in the first case or to start the second scene half way into the argument at the table an hour later.

If the scene has additional purpose – that is it adds to the screenplay either in terms of character, foreshadowing, atmosphere, background information, if it sets up more than just the scene to follow, then it may stay.

The question to ask is, if you cut this scene, will it affect the story? If the answer is that it won't, you may not need it.

If the answer is yes, can you combine it with another scene?

Description 101

Keep the description terse, sharp, short. Regarding the action, ask yourself, *Is it necessary?* How much time will it take a camera to every detail you've described, do all of the details add to the scene? If there is dialogue, make sure it fits the pace of the scene and doesn't slow it down.

Make sure each scene has a predicament

The main issue with scenes that don't work in a script, regardless of how clever or witty or beautiful they may be, is when there is no real predicament. Nothing happens; nothing is at stake.

I'm not talking in terms of major action or revelation, but your character's life should not be the same at the end of a scene as it was at the start, even if the change is minuscule and not recognised by the characters yet.

Scene clichés: avoid or re-imagine

Waking up to an alarm clock is inexcusable!

Unless the 'alarm clock' is a small child who has been trained to stand by the bed at 6.45 am and go, 'Beep beep'.

Similarly, waking up from a dream at the end of the script has been inadmissible ever since Bobby Ewing stepped out of the shower in Dallas. If you don't know the reference, just ask anyone in their fifties.

Every genre has its own characteristic tropes and visual clichés. If you are writing in a particular genre, study the tropes that are specific to it. Know which ones will work for your story and what you can subvert – thus surprising your readers whose expectations are angled by the genre to expect something else to happen. Then you are using them for a good and effective purpose.

Clichés are also sometimes permissible if they allow you to get your story moving quickly. If it's a faster way to get to get the story firing along and hook us, you may be forgiven. Otherwise, it's lazy writing.

Exercises

1. Visual storytelling

Take this description: *Alice approaches. She is someone Frank fears.*

Now rewrite the second sentence into action. How can you show how Frank feels? Exactly how afraid is he? What would he do to avoid (or remove himself) from this encounter? Will there be an encounter?

What you decide to show will depend on location, the age of the characters and the position of the scene within your story's structure. Frank might move quickly out of sight, drop the books he's carrying, try frantically to pick them up off the ground while avoiding eye contact, walk away quickly and bump into Alice in his confusion. Maybe he apologises (almost for existing) or starts talking rapidly about shooting stars or the anatomy of bees to cover up his fear or even fall on his knees and pray to strange gods.

Would Alice stop? Does she know how Frank feels or is she oblivious? If she knows, how does this make her feel - all powerful or confused or apologetic? Maybe he fears her because of her big brother or her father or their families' ongoing feud/ debt, etc.

2. Introducing character

Take a character and think of three ways to answer this question: If you have 15 seconds to introduce this character, what do you need to reveal to your readers? What do they need to know *now* and how will you reveal it?

What can she be doing that will make her memorable? Something that will resonate with her personality, life, the world you are authenticating or a trait that will be relevant later on. Something we will find intriguing or visually interesting?

3. Location

Look around the room you're in. How would you describe it, if you could only include three aspects of the space? Use colour, sound, music, time of day, background noise, crowded or not, public or not, lighting, texture.

Now do the same again but this time you want the space to seem scary or intimidating, then warm and friendly.

4. Sound and space

Background noise can create an atmosphere. Take a location you're thinking of using in your script. Consider the sounds that could be in the location, in the background or foreground and sounds that might filter in from outside the location. Which of these could you use to create an atmosphere within the scene you're planning or to have an impact on your characters' moods?

Are there people talking or a radio playing off screen? If so, what type of music or voices might they be - loud, soft or argumentative? What other sounds might we hear? Birdsong, a Hoover, a mouse in the woodwork, a cockroach crushed underfoot – all can help create an atmosphere that will help your scene.

If you want to make a scene feel claustrophobic, would you make it small, dark, hot, crowded, use disturbing music or cartoons on a loop from a screen behind the sofa? What sounds would disturb your central character?

Now, how would you use sound to make the same location romantic or fun?

5. Action and dialogue

Take all the dialogue out of a scene you've written and see if you can tell the story of that scene without it. Use gesture, silence, movement, behaviour.

Then put back in *only* the lines of dialogue that you really need.

15: Other Aspects of Scene Writing

"The job of the dramatist is to make the audience wonder what happens next. Not to explain to them what just happened or to 'SUGGEST' to them what happened."

– David Mamet

Handling exposition

Exposition is the information we need:

- for the story to move forward
- for readers to understand the goal, motivation and mindset of your characters
- for readers to understand the impact of certain actions and events on character or plot.

Not everything needs to be revealed

This is very important to remember. You have a limited time to tell your story but readers are smart and your characters are real. Think of exposition as ammunition. You target your readers with information that is powerful and has an impact on the story and on how we feel about your characters.

How you do this: by only revealing information your readers desperately want to know.

And then only when they need to know

The trick is to reveal the information in a way that avoids your readers feeling they are being told something that the writer feels is important. Pure information-giving is boring. You need to find a way to get it across without *telling* us.

Use what you have created to reveal the information we need: character, location and events.

Just taking character: what if your character knows something she will never reveal in a million years, how do you make it possible for us to find out what she knows? One trick is to engineer an emotional response that allows or forces her to blurt it out. You might write the scene so that she loses her temper or loses heart; she might reveal the information to hurt the other person, to prove a point or because she's tired of being the strong, silent one, of pretending to be someone she isn't.

Maybe it comes out unintentionally under the influence of drink, because she thinks everyone already knows, because someone is dying or has died, because she wants to shock, hurt or impress the other person, because she's lost and afraid?

Keep revelations to a minimum

Draw us into the story first and make us care. We don't need to know everything, especially at the start of the script. Then, when you reveal what we need to know, either for the plot or to make us care more about your characters, we will be ready for it.

Timing

A piece of information about a character or a clue to the story's resolution will work differently depending on where you place it.

Let's say we open with a detective breaking into a room and finding a witness has hanged himself. The emotional power of this scene – forgetting for a moment the impact that the actual staging of the scene will have, depending on the style and desires of the writer – will be different if it is the opening scene, the catalyst, the midpoint, the second turning point or a plot point placed somewhere else along the route.

In terms of exposition, let's look at a few choices you might consider:

- If we already know that this detective, your central character, found her father dead in the same way when she was eight, we will be watching to see how she will deal with this discovery. Does she become an automaton determined to find the person responsible/ break down/ go absent without leave? How she responds will depend on what's best for your story.

- How and when did we find out about this incident in her past? What if the story she told or that we have learnt isn't true? Maybe she had the opportunity to save her father but didn't take it and why? Could this be the secret/ flaw that she has to admit at the end of Act 2? What if she was trapped in the room with her dead father for days? What age was she when it happened?

- If her colleagues know, do they try to prevent her going in? Is this how we find out (some version of) her backstory? Is the case taken off her and we only find out what happened to her in the past because she has to fight to keep it?

- What if we know *nothing* of this aspect of her backstory? Yet.

- What if she has lied? Consistently or when pushed for information? What if she claims to go visit her father every weekend or that her parents abandoned her? If her behaviour after she find this body hints at an issue and we gradually realise that is issue is a serious flaw for her and yet you choose only to reveal where it came from (her backstory, or part of it) later, will this do more (or less) for our identification with your central character or for the story?

Key questions

Essentially, there are two key questions to consider with exposition:

- What do people need to know and when?
- Do they need to care first?

Role of subtext

Subtext is the content or meaning that lies beneath what's said or done in a scene. It's the element that isn't revealed at this point, when we know there is more beneath the surface than meets the eye.

In a screenplay, it is always related to character. As such, subtext can apply to and enrich any character in your script. It especially relates to the backstory or interior struggle of your central character to choose the most appropriate solution to her interior conflict.

If it is built properly into your storyline, subtext increases the urgency for your central character to make a choice at pivotal moments. Subtext brings us into her dilemma and helps us understand it. For example, if life is repeating itself and she must act to end the cycle, somehow.

The subtext does not have to be revealed but avoid things that appear arbitrary. For example, it makes more sense in the teen sniper scenario (see Chapter 10), that your central character was trained to use a gun after her parents were assassinated because she was also a potential target. Almost more importantly, she avoids all contact with guns. We may be aware of this but if she is in denial of the event(s) that led to her being in this position or is unable (or unwilling) to explain why she feels that way, it becomes subtext.

Then it is up to you to decide how much of that reason you want or need to foreshadow but also whether to eventually reveal it to us and when.

Creating False Situations of Scarcity

This is where you design a scene location, environment or elements within that scene to make it impossible for your character to do or say something they are set on doing or saying.

Alternatively, the scene's design will force her to do or say something she never meant to say or do, for dramatic or comic effect. Essentially, you are ensuring that you get the end result you need from your scene, both emotionally and in terms of story or character.

At its extreme, you might take two people who do not want to be near each other, may even *need* not to be near each other and you stick them in a car that breaks down in rush hour traffic.

Be creative and have fun; this is where you play devil's advocate – finding not the best thing that will help your character but creating circumstances that actively work against her. What if your central character has promised to reveal something important when she meets her friend, but it's a public place and they can be overheard so she clams up? What if she's about to speak when a birthday party spills in or they get dragged into a hen night? An ex appears and corrals her into conversation so the opportunity is lost?

Better, instead of revealing something, maybe she ends up lying to her friend, leading to further complications.

You are creating artificial 'walls' around your character to force choices or action that work against what she wants in favour of your story.

Let's say your character wants to propose to her girlfriend that they move in together. She's managed to catch up with her at the bus shelter, only it's full of people because it's raining. Before she can say what she came to say, a dog pees on her leg. She kicks the dog; her girlfriend is disgusted that she did this and lets her know.

Before they know it, they're having the row to end all rows and possibly the relationship. The bus comes. The girlfriend gets on.

Your character ends up in a place she never intended to be, story-wise.

And she's wet.

It's false because you've manufactured elements of that scene to put pressure on character. But that's what plot is. By creating an obstacle to a character's needs (the setting, the weather, attitudes, witnesses) in that scene, you have created conflict (the row) and a resulting issue or problem that will have to be overcome: are they even talking to each other anymore?

Voiceover/ narration

When it works, it can be spectacular. It's a distant voice imposing a viewpoint outside the story world you've created. It may or may not be your central character. When it isn't needed, it can be seen as lazy writing that allows the writer to explain the story or tells us what we are seeing.

So how can you judge whether you need it in your screenplay?

Does the voiceover run all the way through the script or are you using it as a device to set-up a character/ story?

The basic rule of thumb is that if you use it at the start, you should use it throughout. If you only use it for a certain section of your script, you may be able to do without it. If you can find another way to reveal the same information, to create the same atmosphere, you may not need it. I have written scripts where I've ended up taking out voiceover after I'd finished the first draft. Initially, I needed it to help me get into the head of the central character and her world but then I was able to do without it.

Does it reveal something other than what we see on screen?

If it contradicts what we're seeing or describes it in a way that jars, then it is working. For example, if the narrator tells us her childhood was blissful but we see her having her head held down in a bucket of water by her mother, then we're intrigued or concerned.

Does voiceover make your story stronger?

Voiceover can be a powerful device when, for example, it plays with our expectations and understanding of what we are seeing on screen. For example, if a character commits a violent crime on screen while describing it in voiceover or narration as if it were a scene in a fairytale.

Juxtaposition

This is when you cut between fragments of scenes or between sequences to draw attention to some aspect of the story and character being revealed. You are manipulating your reader's emotions by comparing or contrasting what's happening in each scene or sequence.

For example, in *Michael Collins*, Neil Jordan cuts back and forth between the 'love scene' between Collins and Kitty (Julia Roberts) in the Gresham during the early hours of the morning in which he has sent his men to assassinate the British spies led by Soames (Charles Dance).

The impact of the passive sequence in the hotel where they reveal their love for each other, coupled with his knowledge of what is happening outside (which he will not talk about, thus creating additional subliminal conflict within the scene) contrasts visually with the very real and life-changing horrors that his men are facing.

Juxtaposing scenes that are so different in tone and pace draws attention to that horror in a way that running the love scene on its own after or in the middle of the sequence of killings wouldn't.

Flashback

Flashbacks should be used with caution. Like voiceover and narration, there's a rule of thumb that if you use flashback once, it should be a device you use throughout your film. (See tip below.) An exception to this, but also a way to avoid flashbacks later, is by opening with the event in the past and then switching forward into the present time/ aftermath.

Then there is also the question of where you use them. As a rule, you don't want to use flashbacks in Act 1. We need to know and care about your central character before you take us backwards into her life.

Flashbacks do seem to work within films in which an incident is gradually truthfully recalled over the course of a film. For example, if a character believes she was responsible for her brother's death at the start of the screenplay but then, as the story progresses, she recalls more of the actual incident. Eventually, she remembers that there was a third party in the boat and finally that this person killed her brother. (And was the person who had convinced her of her guilt all those years earlier.)

The temptation is to rely on flashbacks to give us access to your central character's thoughts/ memories/ perspective on events while allowing us to also see what happened; at least as she remembers it happening. That can give us emotional insight into a character but it may also necessitate the casting of younger versions of existing characters (and additional characters), not to mention additional scene set-ups and lighting for a few moments of screen time.

> Tip: To see if your flashbacks work, take them all out of your script and join them together. They should work like a short film in which there is momentum, a story that starts and concludes.

How you might avoid flashbacks

Flashbacks effectively stop your story's momentum by pulling readers back in time to explain or illustrate something. Explaining through a visual scene is still giving us information. As with any scene, work out what you want us to get from your flashback. Once you know its purpose, you may be able to find other, more creative ways to let us know this information, without going back to that moment in the past.

Let's say you want to show that a father misses the relationship he had with his son. Searching for his now adult and homeless son, the father passes a waste-ground. Maybe there's a football match happening and you insert a flashback of him playing football with his young son to show how he misses the relationship they had when his son was a child.

Knowing what you want to achieve with the scene, here's a non-flashback alternative: the father sees another dad kicking a ball with his young son and stops for a moment to watch. It's all in that moment when his sense of loss throws him for a beat. He doesn't even realise the boy is yelling at him to throw back the ball.

Or maybe the scene concludes because the kid points out the strange staring man to his dad. Because we know the man is looking for his adult son, we understand what has happened without the writer needing to show us a specific memory. We feel for him because we are present with him.

Take the scene from *In Name Of The Father* when Gerry's father lands into Gerry's cell. In this scene we learn why their relationship is so flawed. It opens irrationally with Gerry accusing his father of, "always following me when I do something wrong". According to Gerry, he decided to be bad when he was a child and it's all because of a football match. Gerry had cheated but his team had won for the first time in their lives. His father followed him around asking him if he'd fouled the ball.

Everyone laughed at his father.

The upshot of the incident was that Gerry decided he might as well be bad. There is so much in that scene for the young Gerry – everyone was laughing at his father, his father had been right, the need to win at something once, the sense of guilt, of not being able to live up to his father's ethical standards.

The temptation would be to go back and show the incident – but how many scenes would it take to show the match and the aftermath, not to mention setting up an outdoor location and a cast of younger kids?

Besides, what makes it so powerful is that Gerry's father doesn't even remember the incident. Instead of going back in time, we experience the event without leaving the present day. We see that football match and its aftermath in our heads, through Gerry's remembering of it in a prison cell because of where and when it occurs in the screenplay and how much emotion he is feeling.

Sometimes, but rarely, flashbacks can be the most effective way to tell a story. Most of the film *Amadeus* is told in flashbacks although it begins in the present and establishes Salieri in our minds first and his feelings of guilt.

The majority of the film takes place when he knew Mozart so, in actual fact, the writer is using flash-forwards to package his tale. It's worth looking at how he achieved this so seamlessly, both with Mozart's music and with Salieri's body language often mirroring his behaviour in transitions.

Style

Style is not the icing on cake, added after everything else works. However, you can definitely add to it after you have your story working. Ideally, it should intensify the key sensations of the film and be reflected in every line of dialogue or description. It can come from your work on theme or character backstory, as much as from the genre and tone you're looking to create.

Style can also convey important aspects of your plot, characters and momentum allowing your overall story to feel uniquely unified and all enveloping. You could, for example, use an image system throughout your screenplay. (See Exercise 1, below)

It can be as deceptively simple as choosing the right words to evoke powerful images or sensations, to create pace, tone and other atmospheric qualities. All of these can lift your script those few heady inches above all the rest on the producer's desk. It may simply be your voice coming through.

Exercises

1. Image system

An image system is a series of images you use throughout your film that reflect the story.

For example, in *Witness,* there's the image system connected with wheat. To take just a few examples of how this is used: Initially, we see men ploughing a wheat field in the Amish community. Then there is bread at the funeral. No technology has touched the wheat, the flour or the eventual bread. It's pure. Then John Book arrives and his bullets are hidden in a flour canister. The flour is now contaminated by his world. Finally, a wheat silo forms a key moment (and lethal weapon) in the culmination of the story.

Taking your theme, brainstorm images and sounds you connect with it. From the images you come up with, are there any that could form a useful and cohesive or imaginative image system that would add to your script?

For example, if your film is about the triumph of goodness and you come up with the idea of angels, then you have wings, birds, butterflies, feathers (how many types of feathers are there, how many colours, what's that superstition about a feather indicating a death?), road-kill birds, turkeys, (Christmas/ Thanksgiving/ family gatherings/ turkey farm?) hunters, swans, nests, the sound of flapping wings, of birds fighting, birdsong, the dawn chorus, eggs (Easter, cracked eggs, cooking, collecting, breeding birds?).

Could you use any of these to add a layer to your story? It may not be a layer anyone else is aware of, but it can help you tell the story. And, trust me, it's very satisfying!

2. Flashback

If there is a moment in your story when you would like to use flashback to reveal an event in the past, work out exactly what you want your readers to know at the end of it.

Do they need to know everything or *just enough?*

Now, can you find a way to achieve this without using flashback?

3. Voiceover/ narration

- Take a key scene and try it with and without voiceover by the different characters in the scene. It may lead to you describing the scene in a different way when you remove it.
- If you have a scene with voiceover, look at it again. What could you do to tell us what's happening without narration of the event?

16: Script Format

"But the love of a good story, of terrific characters and a world driven by your passion, courage and creative gifts is still not enough. Your goal must be a good story well told."

– Robert McKee

If you want to be taken seriously, your script has to look professional. Therefore, it must be formatted correctly, with no typos, lots of space and numbered pages. And never forget to have accurate contact details on the cover page. You want them to be able to reach you! A sample page is in Appendix A.

MARGINS

The basic rule of thumb with script formatting is that there should be plenty of blank space. Font should be Courier 12 point, most likely in memory of the typed scripts with which this industry began.

Do not cram a page, because if it's difficult to read, you annoy the reader because you make them work too hard.

- A4 Pages.
- One side only.
- Dialogue: 2½ inches in from the left; 6 inches from the right.
- Parenthesis: 3 inches from left; 5½ inches from left.
- Character: 4 inches in from left.
- Action/Description: 1½ inches from left; 7½ inches from right.
- Header: 1½ inches from left; 7½ inches from right.

Header

The HEADER has three elements, all in upper case/ capitals:

> INT/EXT. LOCATION – DAY/NIGHT

The header may or may not be underlined.

> INT, EXT, INT/EXT:

Interior or exterior. If a scene includes both – for example somebody arriving at a house and being shown into the hall, it is put as INT/EXT because both locations will appear in the shot and will have to be lit appropriately.

> LOCATION

Where is the scene set? If one location is used frequently, such as LUNDY'S HOTEL, but different rooms feature in different scenes, then you add the specific room after you've clarified the main location. For example:

> LUNDY'S HOTEL/ LOBBY
> LUNDY'S HOTEL/ BAR

Once you establish a location by name, you must continue to use that tag consistently. For example, ROSEMARY'S BEDROOM should not become BEDROOM or ROSEMARY'S ROOM in other scene headers.

If a single scene moves through many rooms in a single location however, it is possible to put, for example, ROSEMARY'S HOUSE/ VARIOUS and then tell us, as we go, within scene description, which room we are moving into.

> DAY/ NIGHT/ LATER/ CONTINUOUS

Generally this allows cast and crew to know the time period in which the scene is set and allows you to have an overview of your timeline. Even for an indoor scene, it's important to know the time of day as this will affect the amount of light filtering in through the window, possibly suggest background noise.

For example, a suburban environment may be quieter at night, the curtains may be drawn and noisier during the morning when kids are passing on the way to school but you do not need to specify MORNING or EVENING. DAY or NIGHT is enough.

You also do not need to be specific about exact time – as in 12.01am. Your eventual audience will not know it's 12.01am unless you indicate it elsewhere within the actual scene.

CONTINUOUS/ TIME CONTINUOUS can be used for scenes that flow into each other, time-wise.

LATER is used instead of Day/ Night if time has moved on but we haven't moved into a different part of the day and haven't moved location. For example, it is often used for a long scene that is broken into shorter scenes or in which time has passed. The first scene could be the start of a family dinner but the next scene might be during the middle of a row that has erupted, that is *later* in the same setting.

Scene numbers

These are only necessary in your final draft. They can be useful to include when you are sending your script for feedback because it makes it easier to identify which scene you are discussing when it comes to getting notes.

When included, scene numbers go in the left margin of the header and, depending on style, also in the far right.

Line spacing

- Single spacing for dialogue.
- Double space between paragraphs of action.
- Double space between header and action/ description.
- Single space between character and dialogue and between character/ parenthesis and parenthesis/ dialogue.

Description

Next up, generally, is description. This can be action, set or character description. The first time we meet a character in description or action, her name should be capitalised but only that first time. (They never need to be capitalised in dialogue unless the name is being shouted.)

There is no need for all description to be in capitals but some writers capitalise every sound, for example:

```
Eric leaves and the door SLAMS behind him.
```

This is a personal choice but can work well in action-based scripts as it adds a sense of drama or violence.

American producers tend to expect description to head up a scene so that the stage is set before anyone speaks. Some writers like to have a line of dialogue from the previous scene (say Scene 1) in at the top of the next scene (Scene 2) as voiceover, to keep the script flowing.

Keep description brief, but ensure that you describe whatever is happening as it will be seen on the screen. Too much description, *no matter how well written*, can slow down the script and distract from the story. (See Chapter 14.)

You want the script to be easy to read so write with a view to having lots of space by breaking the action into beats, each deserving of its own paragraph.

Camera instructions

Avoid. They get between the reader and your story. If you want readers to engage with your story, why put technical jargon in their way? There is the risk, possibly apocryphal, that your director could decide to do something different simply because she doesn't want to be told how to film your scene.

Your role as the writer is to write in a way that suggests everything you need to be captured on the screen.

Parentheses/ Speech direction

These are the bracketed and italicised directions under a character's name that instruct an actor on how to deliver a particular line or speech: For example, *regretfully, with a smile, playfully* and so on.

Use with extreme caution.

Trust the characters you have created. How their dialogue will play should be clear from the scene, from your description of her entering the scene (and/or from what has happened before) or from the dialogue itself.

Where direction is necessary is if it is possible to have more than one interpretation of the speech or if it is being delivered in a way that contradicts the speech, for example, *sarcastically*.

Do not use parenthesis for movement or reaction. Also, if your direction goes beyond one line in the parenthesis margins, it probably should be out in the action margins instead. (See below.)

Movement within scene

Do not put one character's directions within another character's speech. Double space and bring it out to the description/ action margins. For example:

```
                    JANE
        Hey, why didn't you tell me you wrote
        scripts!?


    Mark crosses to the window, hiding his smile.


                    JANE
        I mean, this is a masterpiece!
```

If, however, the character who is speaking moves, but continues to speak after the move, then you can pull that movement into the description/ action margins but you do not necessarily have to retype the character's name if they continue speaking.

For example:

```
                    JANE
     Hey, why didn't you tell me you wrote
     scripts!?


  Jane waves the script in Mark's face.


  This is a masterpiece!
```

Spelling/ grammar

Why prejudice a reader/ producer with a script full of typos? Pet hates for many readers are when these get mixed up:

- Your (belonging to)/ you're (you are);
- It's (it is)/ its (belongs to);
- There (location)/ their (belonging to)/ they're (they are);
- To (direction)/ too (also).

Don't leave all the spelling to your computer. Words spelt correctly according to your computer's spell checker may mean something entirely different. For example, an *aerial* shot versus an *ariel* shot. Both words are spelt correctly but the second is a type of gazelle.

If you're not sure which one to use, get someone else to read through your script who is good at spotting mistakes. A script free of typos and properly formatted shows you are serious about screenwriting.

Exercise

Take a couple of scraps you've written and type them up in the proper script format. It's much easier to keep going when it looks professional. Using everything you've done so far, give the scene a heading, then a description, then introduce the character or situation and format whatever dialogue or action you have written so far.

Now fill the page and see where it goes. Try it with another scene you've been toying with or with the scene in which we meet your main character for the first time. Play with them and feel good.

17: Who is Your Audience?

"Audiences are harder to please if you're just giving them effects, but they're easy to please if it's a good story."

– Steven Spielberg

Your first audience is the reader. If your script works, readers will feel they are watching it on screen as they turn the pages. You want them glued to the seat, unable to stop until they get to the end; asking questions, intrigued, moved in some way and needing to know what happens next.

But you are ultimately writing for the screen so you have an intended audience for your finished film or TV pilot. Who are you writing your screenplay for? Teens, the grey dollar, children, adults, families? Is it a genre piece with its own target audience?

Then ask yourself, what do you want them to feel at the end of your script?

There are several ways to draw your audience into the story.

Move us: The emotional link

If we care about your characters – care, not necessarily like – we will connect. It's simple human nature. Another way to pull us in to your story emotionally is by giving us something in the story to which we can relate: a universal theme (love, betrayal, fear) or subject (relationship breaking down, moving home/ country/ job).

If something in the plot relates to our lives, we will connect – provided it is handled in a way that feels credible and authentic. On another level we may be interested in the genre and be drawn into your story by that.

The greater our connection, the greater the sense of catharsis we feel when your character succeeds (or fails) at the end.

Excite us: the adrenaline kick

Most of our lives don't contain a huge amount of excitement. Even if they do, we may never have had a chance to take real risks and might not want to, if we're genuinely honest. Films can offer us a way to experience these risks, feel this excitement in safety – through fictional others to whom we relate. Again, this can happen through our connection with your unique characters; what they do or what they take on. Vicariously, we can be a fighter pilot, a drag artist or someone who risks everything to save the world/ her family/ the dog from being put down.

Another way to excite us is through the story itself. A script set in a dystopian world, on a distant galaxy or during an historic event; the possibility of invasion, of an intergalactic battle or medical disaster or just a love story set against extreme odds.

Whatever the story, however, the screenplay still has to build momentum to keep us hooked and invested in what happens next.

Surprises and reverses, the style of writing, the tone of the dialogue, all of these can stimulate us as readers and viewers. Whatever makes this film different will excite us, provided you can maintain the credibility of your world and your story narrative.

Teach us something: the sociological lesson

Every film has an ending, generally with all the questions (or most of them) resolved in some way. This, in itself, is satisfying. It's probably why films or TV series that deliberately don't resolve the central issue(s) – and not just the TV series *Twin Peaks or Lost* or the David Lynch film, *Mulholland Drive* – can leave the general audience dissatisfied. The plot isn't tying things up in a way we expect.

It might seem simplistic but, in theory, we can learn how to deal with universal issues that affect us daily through film. How to handle arguments or conflict, how to survive divorce, how to open up about concerns and issues or how to talk to our kids/ parents can all be side benefits of watching films.

If the characters on screen manage to survive against the odds, we experience a sense of relief, even triumph.

But for that to work, their journey can't be easy.

Exercise

While pitching is a virtual art form in itself and crucial for selling your script, until you have your first draft written, it's not something you need to worry about. However, it's really useful to have a think about how you will eventually do this.

Here are a few points to consider, even at this early stage. You never know when you might meet someone who asks you what you're working on. Pitch it right and they might show an interest. That interest might be enough motivation to push you to finish your script sooner than you might otherwise have managed.

1. Your film:

Title: It shouldn't be necessary to read the whole script to understand.

Target audience: Who are your ideal viewers? Is it for TV or the big screen?

What are your story's unique selling points (USPs)? Some questions to consider might be:

Can you reference other films? You don't want to be the same or even to aim at copying a popular film but you can combine different films to indicate the genre and tone.

Does it deal with a universal issue specific to this target group?

How different it is to what has gone before and what's your special angle?

2. How will your screenplay attract an audience?

Will your story/ character:

Move us?

Excite us?

Teach use something useful?

18: Getting The Pages Down: Productivity Tips

"Writing is the art of applying the seat of your pants to the seat of your chair."

– Ernest Hemingway

Writers are always being asked how many hours they work, whether they sit at the desk from nine to five or allow themselves to skive off from time to time. (We do, it's what keeps us slightly sane. Sometimes.) Every writer has to find the technique that works for him or her. The playwright Bernard Farrell once told me he wrote for the same 9-5 hours he'd got used to when he worked for a ferry company.

But he added that yes, he was still working when he walked the dog for hours on the beach or gazed out the window.

So let me explode the myths you may have encountered lurking at the back of your brain. These may be stopping you from doing the work now.

There is no perfect time

You may not be able to write every day - but yes, you can. Ten minutes in the loo, when you're out having a smoke, at the bus stop, on the bus.

There is no perfect place

You can plot or think about your character's defining moments or attitudes as you drive or cycle, while you wait to collect your child from a grind or while your food cooks. Mind you, I have burnt quite a lot of food this way. (It's good to set a timer.)

Writing is a muscle

If you want to get better at it, you have to put the time in. But, be comforted: it's impossible to write brilliant material every time you sit down. Expecting to write rubbish sometimes, maybe even for a prolonged period, makes it easier to sit down and make yourself write.

Think of it as getting rid of the bad writing that's cluttering up your brain so that the good stuff can flood out.

In light of that, here are some of the techniques I have found that help:

Mini-Tasking

I was once advised to write my list of 'writing to dos' on a Friday afternoon for the week ahead. There's less pressure then to work over the weekend but, oddly, you might find you manage to get a few bits done, just to get ahead.

But be realistic.

How much time do you have?

If it's limited, break your writing task down into parts. Pages, even. Divide it into pieces that are doable in ten or twenty minutes. (And always include a few tasks that you have already done; we may be fooling ourselves but it's nice to tick several things off after you've achieved your first task on the Monday!)

It's better to have small fragments of work that are achievable. Promise yourself that you will write one page of a scene or half a page of dialogue per day and you know it's possible. Then, on certain days, when you do twice this amount (or more), you will feel so much more positive about your progress than if initially expected to write ten pages a day straight off.

Once you get into the habit of doing a little bit regularly, without being too tough on yourself to come up with something amazing, you'll find you need to do it or will miss it when you don't.

The Ten-Minute Snatch

Ten minutes. Every day. Find time. Turn off your phone. Let your coffee go cold. Set a timer and then take one scene, one character, one idea and force and force yourself to write something about it.

Don't expect gems, just do the writing. Watching scraps of paper build up is a good feeling. It's turning you into a writer. Creativity is an unpredictable mistress and sometimes it is a matter of making yourself put words on a page and hoping creativity will show up because she hates to miss out. She's a curious beast.

When you have time, type these fragments up on the computer. They will grow, change, lead to different scene ideas. The fact that you are writing in odd places, at odd times means that you will come up with material you might not find if you had a quiet scheduled hour to write, although such hours will be gold once you're in the thick of the script.

I often find breakthroughs come or I write some really exciting scenes when I genuinely don't feel like doing anything. Although, I have to admit that this might only happen right at the end of that ten minutes.

Arrive early for meetings

Another trick is to arrive 30 minutes early for a meeting and use this time to write.

I have heard of a writer who has a different technique for ensuring he puts the time in. He straps himself into his chair with a belt. The logic is that if he tries to get up, the belt stops him momentarily. So he decides to give it another few minutes, to finish that page, the next paragraph, one more task.

Chocolate, crisps and stopping short

While I find bribing myself to write one more page with the promise of chocolate, crisps, another cup of coffee or a chance to check up on social media, can work, other writers swear by leaving their work mid-scene or mid-sentence. It's easier to get back into the work because they simply have to finish that sentence or scene to be back in their writing world.

The rule of nine

I don't work 9-5, I have no set routine and I almost always work evenings and weekends or sneak into the office when everyone's quiet or occupied. I write in every room of the house, often following the sun and heat, rather than limiting myself to the room I'm meant to be writing in. I'm also an expert at procrastination until a deadline looms. (I set myself a lot of deadlines!)

As I said above, I frequently burn food because I've snatched a few minutes while something cooks. I've even burnt things I didn't think were possible to burn! But the main thing that has helped me get work done in the last few years is a nine-day writing cycle.

A little knowledge can be a dangerous thing but in this case, used for creating self-imposed deadlines, it has proven very useful; albeit this is probably not in the way the knowledge itself was intended. It comes from numerology, about which I know next to nothing except this: essentially, you can reduce every day to a number between 1-9. You do this by adding all the day's digits together (year, month and date) and adding them again until you end up with a single figure.

So the day on which I'm writing this is 11 December 2017. That would be 11 + 12 +2017. Add them all together: 2 + 3 + 10 = 25. Keep adding them to each until you get a single figure, in this case 7.

Every day apparently has a certain value in terms of what works well on that day but all that I really use for my work are days that add up to the numbers 1, 3 and 9. Let it be said, I use these as a helpful writing tool and the numerical value of a day will not prevent me from doing anything on that day!

1, 3 and 9

As might be expected, a '1' day is all to do with beginnings. It's good for starting a project or a phase of a project.

Days that add up to the number '3' are reputedly good for creativity and communication. In my mind, I often save these for days when I need to crack a difficult issue in a script or story, to brainstorm a way out of a hole or for just having fun with an idea.

Then you have the '9' days. Again, as you might expect, this is a day for completion. For me, that's the important aspect of the nine-day cycle. It gives me a deadline. I try to complete whatever piece of work I have set as my task within the 9 days.

Nine days is simply a more realistic span of time, given commitments that suddenly appear and urgent work that leaps onto your lap making mewling sounds and refusing to be ignored. It's not too long and it's not too short. What I have found is that having a cycle of nine days to get work done is simply more effective than giving myself a week. I can even, sometimes, take weekends off (in theory!).

The added bonus is that when one month turns into the next, you can sometimes get a really long 'nine' day cycle. If, for example, the last day of the month adds up to an '8' (such as 31 December 2017) then the first date of the new month (1 January, 2018) will add up to a '4'. You won't reach the next '9' day until 6 January, 2018, giving you a total of 14 days in which to complete a piece of work.

Exercise

The map of productivity

Take an A4 page and put it sideways. Divide it into six with lines. Each of the boxes represents stuff you need to do. You are compartmentalising it so that there are items you can tick off, knowing you are making progress.

In the top three, write an aspect of the project you'd like to do. Divide them into smaller tasks. Tiny tasks, even. Tasks such as spending ten minutes developing your central character, brainstorming obstacles leading to a plot point, researching the clothes and culture of the era or typing up two pages of notes.

In the three boxes below, you can have everything else. Keep one for practical tasks that you need to do but can do when you no longer have the space to write: walking the dog, buying food, washing your hair. In another you might list all the people whose emails you need to answer. In the third, it might be research or searches you want to do online.

Some of these tasks you can do when other people are around, when you're tired or less motivated to write. The point of compartmentalising all you'd like to do is that it allows you to see what you can do on your script now and what you need to prioritise.

19: Creating Your Own Inspiration

"Writing, like all creative expression, for all its struggle, represents in the end a kind of structured, organised, orchestrated dreaming. The writer's most basic task – before tale, before character and dialogue – is to learn how to let himself dream in a free yet orderly fashion."

- Richard Walter, screenwriter, UCLA

Mind Mapping

Mind mapping uses free association to allow you to explore your theme, story or character(s) in more depth and without your imagination being censored! You can do it for a particular moment you are having trouble with or even for a word that's key to your story or a character. There are various ways to do this but essentially, there are no rules. This is about freeing up your mind to do some of the things it does best – to remember and imagine.

It's not about trying to be logical.

- Write a key word from your theme in the middle of a page. An A3-sized page is great. The larger the page, the more freeing and fun it is and sometimes that can bring out the best ideas.
- What are the words that come to mind when you think of this word? Jot these down at random. Then, whatever words they make you think of and whatever words those words make you think of, and so on.
- Next, think of sounds, textures, memories, smells, colours that you associate with these words; people, names, places that might have a connection, however tenuous or odd.

- When you run out of space, take a word that resonates onto another page and start again. See what images, sounds, colours and memories it evokes take a word.

What you write is meant to be random. It doesn't have to make sense. You're stimulating your mind to come up with unexpected images and ideas; to surprise you. You might have ten minutes or half an hour and the more you do it, the easier it gets.

> TIP: use colour pens or markers. Apparently this is a way to trick your brain into thinking you're not actually working but having fun. As a result, it will more easily access material you might not consciously find.

Sensory clusters

- Take an emotion that is central to your story, for example grief, happiness, anger. Without over-thinking it, write down the first colour you associate with the word.
- Leaving the original word to one side, focus on the colour and list five objects that come to mind when you think of this colour.
- Now list five sounds you'd associate with this colour, five places, five smells, five textures.
- Let's say the emotion you chose was 'grief' and it gave you the colour yellow. Maybe yellow then gave you laughter, sunshine, balloons, the smell of roses, a carousel. How could you use some of those elements in a scene to illustrate grief? Using the elements you came up with, challenge yourself to think of a scenario involving some or all of these that would illustrate a character's experience of the emotion with which you began the exercise, whether they can show it or not, whether they are in denial or only now discovering how strongly they feel.

It will be unlike any scene you could have logically thought up to show this emotion.

The 'Noticings' notebook

Take a notebook and make yourself write down one observation every day – about people, animals, the weather, the shape a branch of leaves makes in the wind, the sound of a child whining/ laughing/ snoring/ asking a question over and over.

One tiny thing. Every day.

Once it becomes a habit, build up to two or three.

Don't worry if you miss a day or you haven't the notebook to hand, write them on scraps of paper you can stick into the notebook later. Or on your phone. The back of your hand. Your knees if you have torn jeans!

This isn't for literary purposes or for anyone else's eyes. It's simply to train yourself to see things differently. That child's voice might be really useful off screen in a scene of your film, but so could the clapping sound that bird made flying out of the tree above you or the way someone fluffed up her hair when she took off her woolly hat.

Babysitting

Don't leave your characters at home. Take them with you. Question them. Ask yourself whatever questions spring to mind:

- If my character was on the bus with me, what would she being doing/ thinking?
- If the bus was marooned on a desert island, who would she befriend, how would she cope?
- What is she unhappy about now?
- What could I do that would really annoy her?
- What is she thinking of when she looks out this window?
- What would she think of me?

Rituals

Rituals can be very useful in charting your character's increasing desperation or loss of control. At one extreme, there are rituals involved around public events, such as weddings, funerals, christenings, Halloween, Christmas, Thanksgiving, New Year's Eve and those focussed on private family gatherings, such as Sunday dinners, anniversaries and birthdays.

These are fantastic excuses for bringing characters together when you need to bring things to a head or reveal the dynamic between characters that can't necessarily be acknowledged because of the setting.

At the farthest end are the private rituals. Because they are personal, they reveal character and you can use them to show how your character is changing, for better and for worse. For example, if your protagonist always has a very smooth and efficient breakfast: coffee on, sings her 'happy song' while she squeezes fresh orange juice and heats her croissant in the oven, has it with homemade jam and fresh butter, walks the dog before she goes to work. Maybe she always kisses her partner goodbye or combs her hair a hundred times before she gets into bed.

When life starts falling apart, these elements will start going wrong, being skipped. She forgets to put coffee or water in the coffee machine, she's out of oranges, runs out of time to walk the dog or the dog has chewed her shoes and so on.

If life is getting better, perhaps you show it by how relaxed she has become about her morning routine, or how she's moving to hot chocolate instead of coffee? Alternatively, maybe she sleeps it out, forgets to brush her hair or snaps the brush in half.

A ritual shows us an element of your character.

Let's say a couple always read their horoscopes to each other while drinking hot chocolate on St Valentine's Day. When this relationship falls apart or no longer exists, for whatever reason, how powerful would it be to see your central character telling her friends that she has plans for the night.

Then she closes the door, make two hot chocolates and reads out both horoscopes to herself.

Look at your main character and think of the public and private rituals that might belong to her day. Experiment with how these might change over the course of your script. Some of them may ultimately belong outside your script but experimenting with how a central character does things in her daily life - be it in public or in private - will help you discover more about who she is. Something will emerge that will be useful and enrich your script.

Finally, unofficial essentials

- Switch to coffee. Cold coffee tastes better than cold tea – and you can zap it. Or at least herbal tea.
- Develop an ability to gaze out windows for long periods and a thick neck. You have to believe that this is work. It might not even feel like work but still.
- Be prepared to be feel manic, depressive and mildly schizophrenic all at once. At least, such skills help. Manic when it's going brilliantly, depressed when the writing really isn't progressing at all and mildly schizophrenic when all the characters you have created feel more real to you than the people you know and love in daily life.
- Oh and stamina. Lots of that.

This is what it is about.

Nobody said it would be easy weaving magic.

20: Post-phew: When you Finish your Script

For 40-odd years in this noble profession
I've harboured a guilt and my conscience is smitten.
So here is my slightly embarrassed confession –
I don't like to write, but I love to have written.

- Michael Kanin

Conventional wisdom says that if you are at a loss – and let's face it, the blank page can be intimidating – you type FADE IN at the top of the page. I think only one of the dozens of scripts I've written actually began with a FADE IN!

Instead, why not write a header such as:

```
INT. KITCHEN — NIGHT
```

At least now you've started a scene and you may continue out of curiosity. You might decide to write a line describing some aspect of this kitchen like the pot boiling over, the rat lying decapitated in the sink or a pair of discarded shoes, red and covered in mud, sitting by the back door.

What else can we see or hear?

- The wind hammering the window frame?
- The sound of an argument off screen?
- A child sitting at the table counting backwards while waiting to be fed?
- Who speaks first? Does anyone speak?
- Is there anyone in this house at all?
- What happens next?

Sometimes, however, the blank page or screen is the wrong the place to start. If so, take a scrap of paper and brainstorm three possible plot points or obstacles and a character trait. See where these might lead. Make your character describe to you how they feel to her. Make her react to them.

When you have a few scraps, type them up. Now you have begun your script. It doesn't matter where in the script those scenes or snatches of description will end up. If you put them into the proper format for a screenplay, they will suddenly seem better too!

I tend to scribble down notes, ideas and lines that could become a scene or might get me into the head of a character on scraps of paper and store them up like a magpie. Sometimes they're spontaneous. Other times, I make myself come up with something, to try and find a way to describe a character or force myself to write a scene, even if I know it doesn't read right. I'll do it over coffee, when I'm out walking, having breakfast, waiting for someone.

You never know where they will lead. When I type up these scraps, sometimes days or weeks later, something good often comes. Even from the ropey bits! Occasionally, though, they will just be ropey bits – but at least they are out of your head now, leaving room for better material to brew.

What if you write an opening image instead? Or allow yourself to brainstorm a scene that is in your head onto the page or screen? Then maybe you can play with the scene that comes before and after? Or dive into a scene that will make you cry or laugh? Jot down situations that you could put character into and see where they lead. Write down three possible places where your story could start and do a scene for each.

Which character will we meet first and when/ where/ why?

You could even write the ending.

The point is, put words down on a page. Then format them so they look like a script and you have begun.

Silence that inner critic

Everything can be fixed. That's the rewriting part and this is your first draft. You can't rewrite any script until you've got the story down. On screen or on paper. Even if there are huge gaps as you go or if scenes seem to be full of dialogue and little else. Don't be afraid to put the words down or to force yourself to write when you really don't want to. Nobody needs to see any of this until you are happy with it.

You write regardless and you fill the pages and you finish your script, page by page, scene by scene. If a particular scene feels too tricky to do today, jot down what you'd like to happen – even a few bullet points or the line from your outline where the scene ends and move on. Write a different scene from later in your story.

Writing every day gives you confidence but you do have to demand that time of yourself and of others. Maybe even postpone other pleasures until the first draft is done. Granted, some days the writing will feel so poor that you will doubt whether you should be writing at all, but that's part of the process.

Get the story down.

Finish the script.

Keep reading

While writing, read as many scripts as you can find in different genres and see how those writers have told/ sold their story. Some people will avoid reading anything in their genre in case they accidentally plagiarise, others will drown themselves in it so they are totally immersed. Whatever works for you.

You will find scripts to read all over the net but avoid 'shooting script' drafts. These are the final stage of the process, when cast and locations are set so there may be very little detail in them that is useful to you as a writer. Join a writing group or set one up. Volunteer to read other people's scripts.

When you finish

When you finish your first draft, you will feel wonderfully self-satisfied. Satiated. Bear this in mind. Think 'cat lying in a sunny spot exhausted from playing with a ball of wool and eating the best meal ever' and you're coming close.

Tired and elated.

And you should. In 21 years of teaching screenwriting, so many students have told me they would finish their scripts and so few have.

What you have done is nothing short of awesome.

Even knowing that it will need more work to make it work as the strongest screenplay it can be, that does justice to your story and ambition, this is the moment to congratulate yourself.

But don't send it out. Not yet. (See Bonus chapter: **The Art of Rewriting**.)

The buzz vs the block

As somebody who gave up a career in journalism to be a full-time screenwriter, screenwriting is an exhilarating form in which to write. The buzz when you find the right way to show a character, a scene that just clicks and propels you and your story forward, when a character begins talking to you in your sleep, when you write scene after scene without needing to think about it. There's nothing like it.

But blocks will happen.

It's highly possibly you'll be overwhelmed by the size of the task at some point. It happens to us all. Step back, remember why you wanted to do this, take a section and focus only on that. The first ten minutes. One crucial scene. Introducing a character. You keep putting the words down until you feel you are making progress.

Or switch to another form of writing and spend some time there. It could be a poem, short story, newspaper article or blog; do something else creative and then return to your script. Or play with some of the exercises in this book and see where they lead.

It does not have to be perfect so keep writing and don't spend hours rewriting what you've already written or thinking it's not good enough. Move on and get to the end. Then you can go back.

Keeping the faith

It is hard work to keep your imagination working.

Sometimes you have to write, without imagination. You put words down, even if it feels like pulling blood from a stone of tiny proportions underwater without oxygen. The words you write can't always be good. But the more you write, the easier it gets and if you leave the rubbish writing inside your head, it might block your imagination from feeding you the gems next time you sit down.

Brainstorm bits and pieces you might use within that tricky scene. What does the location look like? Who might be there apart from your main players? What time of day is it? What sounds can they hear?

Play with the scene. Don't expect it to be perfect or for every detail you come up with to be useful. You're building the scene from the ground up but sometimes it helps to go pick the furnishings first until you're comfortable to lay down the foundations.

Now.

Enough reading.

Start that script. Or finish it. Or do another few scenes in the middle or the end – but get the story down.

Now.

BONUS CHAPTER: The Art of Rewriting

"The road to hell is paved with works-in-progress."

– Philip Roth

When you finish your script – notice I said *'when'* not *'if'* – celebrate your achievement and put it away. For six weeks if you can. Start playing with your next idea and move it forward. You have achieved something most people who say they want to write a script never have and never will.

You have written your first screenplay.

All of it.

You and you alone.

But on the way to this point, understand that most people do not take writers seriously when they are starting out. There is always a certain demand to see results. Ignore this. Or invent an entirely fictional pitch you can pull out when someone asks again and protect the idea you are scripting.

From personal experience, I'd also suggest you don't talk about your idea too much until you have the bulk of it down on paper or on the screen. Many writers will tell you that the stories they keep talking about can be the hardest to eventually write; as if the energy has been dissipated.

Besides, there is little as dispiriting as talking excitedly about the script you're working on only to hear, *"Oh, you're still working on that?"* Unless you have written a screenplay, even if you are a director or a producer, you are unlikely to realise how much work goes into it.

Writing your best script

A good script can be transformed into a bad film but it's very hard to make a good film from a bad script. So your job is to make your script the best it can be. If you write the very best script you can, people will read it.

They can't afford not to.

But that script you submit to the industry won't be your first draft.

That's where the rewriting comes in. Until you are happy that this is the best script you can write at this point, don't send it out for feedback. When you do, make sure you send it to the right person or people. A friend who loves grim crime scripts may not be the person to read a character-driven coming-of-age story, although she may be brilliant on plotting. You could ask her opinion on the plot specifically though.

Not everyone can read scripts

If you're not used to them, they can feel too empty!

The worst thing you can do is show your script to the wrong person, be they friend, family member or industry professional. Take the feedback I got two years after I'd handed over a script to another writer. Mind you, I think the two-year silence was probably a clue as to the feedback I would get.

But I wanted his opinion, even then.

What did he say? *"It was so bad, I didn't know what to say."*

Ouch.

Okay. But I'm professional. I had learnt so much in two years. I told him, *"I agree"*. (Though I had been secretly half hoping it was a work of genius!) Knowing I had become a better writer in the intervening years, I asked if I could give him my new one to read.

"No," he said. *"I probably wouldn't like it."*

Doesn't take a genius to know he wasn't the right person to show new work to!

(And yes the next script was better but I'd blown my chance of him ever looking at it. Granted, he did save me additional heartbreak by being brutally honest about what he thought of my work, past and future, but still.)

So, before you give your new script to *anyone* for feedback, put it away for six weeks if you can. Then take it out, bring it to a cafe or neutral space where you won't bump into anyone you know and read it yourself.

Re-reading your work

When you re-read your script this first time, you are not marking lines or words or scenes that don't work. You're reading for the emotional impact of the whole.

This can be really hard to do, especially in one sitting. You know what you wanted to achieve. You've worked hard to get to this point. While some bits will hum and hit the right note, others will seem too long or too flat. You'll get frustrated with the pace in one part and find it flies along in another. You may hate parts of the script as you read – but don't stop.

This is your first chance to feel the script as a whole.

Most likely, you are being far more critical than you should be, but that's natural. You may even be disappointed in yourself. *Don't be.* Most writers hate first drafts. What professional screenwriters hand out as a 'first draft' may be their fifth or their fifteenth.

Make notes

When you finish reading, make notes. About what you liked and what worked, but also at what points you got easily distracted.

- Are these places that might need work?
- Did any of your characters stop working, make decisions or act in a way that jarred?
- Did something (a scene, an event, a reaction) feel wrong or less than credible?
- Did the plot feel forced at some point or leap ahead, leaving a plot hole in its wake?
- Maybe it dragged a little at some point or the ending is not strong as you thought it was?

What you're listening to now is your gut instinct on where problems may lie. You are likely to feel they are bigger problems than they may be. Keep that in mind as you go through your first draft.

TIP: Make sure you have that piece of paper on which you wrote what the story was about for you and why you wanted to tell this story now. It may be the compass that can direct you, with the distance of six weeks, to know where you need to focus.

The second reading

When you re-read it again, keep these points in mind and watch out for how you can fix them or where they might be triggered as you go through. Don't stop and rewrite. Put marks on the pages or squiggles next to a block of dialogue that feels wooden, an 'x' on a scene or sequence that needs work.

You're just gathering what you need to know. If you start rewriting now, there is a risk that you could destroy what's good in the heat of the moment.

TIP: It can be a good idea to edit a hard copy of your screenplay, rather than editing on the screen. By the time you go to type the changes into your screen version, you may find some of them weren't necessary. Or you may find a better solution.

Gathering feedback

Finally, when you give a script out for feedback, remember that not everyone knows how to read a script. Make it easy for them to give you useful notes. If you simply ask someone if they like your script, that's all they will say.

Yes/No/ sort of won't help you improve your script.

Instead, think about the elements or parts on which you need feedback and ask specific questions:

- Did you care about this character? Why or why not?
- Did you believe she would do this?
- Did the relationships feel credible?
- Was there anything she did or said that you found hard to believe?

Put simply, it's easier to respond constructively to specific questions.

You can also suggest that they respond with their own questions. Questions can be an easier way to give constructive feedback at this tender time. For example, it is harder to be defensive about, *Could he be kinder to her/ more three-dimensional?* than *This character is horrible!*

Look at the notes you get. To make a character more credible might simply mean adjusting some scenes in Act 1, planting (more) clues earlier.

The rewriting process

Once you know the issues you need to tackle in your script, break it into easily achievable pieces. Don't be afraid to brainstorm again, to use your mind mapping tools, to revisit your original notes and find a solution that you might not have seen before. You may prune scenes back or alter characters – provided you are clear in your own mind about what you need to achieve.

Pitch possible solutions to the people who gave you feedback and see how they react.

How you rewrite will depend on you. I've gone back to outline with some, I've taken the storylines out and worked on them individually. That allows me to take parts with me and focus just on them. But once, I rewrote a script three pages at a time, revising from the start of the script each day before rewriting that day's quota. It was slow, it may be my most layered script but it's a technique that requires time and focus.

Whatever way you do it, remember that what you have achieved is amazing. Don't let the rewrite deflate you – it simply means you can now call yourself a screenwriter!

Good luck and keep writing.

Lindsay

APPENDICES

A: Sample Page

INT. FILMBASE/ STUDIO 3 - DAY

The world's most prestigious potential screenwriters
are gathered around the table. A storm RIPS the sky
outside and the lights flicker. Standing at the top
of the room, a TUTOR finishes her multicoloured
drawing of the three-act formula on a flip chart.

One of the students, ELOISE, stabs her pen into the
table.

>   ELOISE
>   *(dramatically)**
>   You can't expect us to obey three-
>   act rules!

Eloise stands up, moves around the table, slowly.

>   ELOISE
>   That would be -

She hesitates, searching for the right word; then
looks up at the TUTOR.

>   ELOISE
>   Murder.

INSERT:

Tattoo on her upper arm that says: **Death to writing
tutors**.

>   CUT TO:

EXT. GRAVEYARD/ FLASHBACK - NIGHT

We are aware of Eloise singing off key.**

                  ELOISE (o.s.)
               *(singing, off-key**)*
        One more tutor, stabbed in Temple
        Bar… One more tutor…

Now we see her, digging calmly.

* This is just an example of where parentheses go - but also how unnecessary they can be. This would be cut since the dialogue shows how she feels.
** Either version would do.

B: Books to Read and Some Online Resources

These are all books that have helped me over the years, a sample from the huge range available. I can remember sitting on the floor of Barnes & Noble on my first visit to New York, surrounded by piles of writing books I wanted to buy and trying to pick just a few.

From these books below, however, nuggets of useful information have woven their way into my screenwriting and from there into my teaching over the past 21 years. I am grateful to them all; except Poetics which (to my shame) did nothing for me but is recognised as the first book on dramatic storytelling/ structure, hence its inclusion here. I have left out publication dates and editions since many have been through so many editions and are also now available as e-books.

Adventures in the Screen Trade: William Goldman. Abacus
Alternative Screenwriting: Dancyger & Rush. Focal Press
Creating Unforgettable Characters: Linda Seger. Samuel French, Hollywood
Image, Sound and Story: Cherry Potter. Martin Secker & Warburg
Making a Good Script Great: Linda Seger. Samuel French Trade, Hollywood
Now, Write! Screenwriting: Edited by S Ellis & C Lamson. Tarcher, Penguin NY
On Writing: Stephen King. Hodder & Stoughton, London.
Raindance Writers' Lab: Write + Sell the Hot Screenplay. Elliot Grove. Focal Press
Screenplay – The Screenwriter's Workbook: Syd Field. Delta Trade Paperbacks, New York

Story: Robert McKee. HarperCollins

The Hero With A Thousand Faces: Joseph Campbell. New World Library

The Writer's Journey – Mythic Structure for Storytellers and Screenwriters: Christopher Vogler. Michael Wiese Productions

The Uses of Enchantment: Bruno Bettelheim, Vintage Books

Writing the Short Film: Patricia Cooper & Ken Dancyger. Focal Press, Boston

Writing Screenplays that Sell: Michael Hauge. Collins

Poetics: Aristotle (translated with an introduction and notes by Malcolm Heath). Penguin Classics, London

For scripts:

Drews script-o-rama (http://www.script-o-rama.com/) and The Daily Script (http://www.dailyscript.com/): Websites with free scripts, often multiple drafts. Always try to avoid the shooting script – the details a writer needed to create a powerful, visual script may not be included because the cast and locations have already been chosen.

BBC Writer's Room (http://www.bbc.co.uk/writersroom): The BBC Writer's Room website, for competitions, scripts and useful information on different genre etc.

C: Hero's Journey

ORDINARY WORLD

CALL TO ADVENTURE
Once raised, time in Ordinary World is running out.

REFUSAL OF CALL (Reluctant hero)
Optional. Some other influence is required to motivate.

MENTOR
Function: to prepare hero to face the unknown

CROSSING THE FIRST THRESHOLD
The story takes off. Your hero finally commits to the adventure/ quest. Having overcome her fear, she decides to confront the problem and take action. There is no turning back.

OVER THE THRESHOLD - TESTS/ALLIES/ENEMIES
Your hero begins to learn the rules of the Special World. She makes major alliances/ enemies/ meets love interest.

APPROACH TO THE INMOST CAVE
We're on the edge of a dangerous place, where the object of the quest is hidden. It may be the HQ of the hero's greatest enemy, for example Hades for Orpheus; the Labyrinth for Theseus.

SUPREME ORDEAL
Your hero's fortunes hit rock bottom. She is in direct confrontation with her

greatest fear and faces possible death. The stakes have risen and so does the tension for your audience: will your hero survive? When she does, we feel elation, exhilaration, catharsis.

REWARD

Your hero takes possession of what she sought, be it an object, knowledge or experience. There is greater understanding (possibly reconciliation) with hostile forces. She may also settle conflict with a parent/ be reconciled with opposite sex; for example in romantic comedy.

THE ROAD BACK

If your hero hasn't yet managed reconciliation with the parent/ gods/ hostile forces, they may come raging after her.

RESURRECTION

Your hero has to be cleansed to return to her world. There is one final life/ death/ supreme ordeal.

RETURN WITH ELIXIR

She returns to her world/ community/ family with the elixir: depending on your story, this may be knowledge, love, freedom, wisdom, experience, some treasure.

~~~

This is only the very briefest of outlines of how the hero's journey works. For more detail on The Hero's Journey see Joseph Campbell: *The Hero with a Thousand Faces*, Christopher Vogler: *The Writer's Journey – Mythic Structure for Storytellers and Screenwriters* but also have a look at Bruno Bettelheim's Uses of Enchantment.

D: Film Bibliography

Alien, screenplay by Dan O'Bannon

Amadeus, screenplay by Peter Shaffer

Blade Runner, screenplay *by* Hampton Fancher and David Peoples, based on Philip K Dick's novel, *Do Androids Dream of Electric Sheep?*

Casablanca: screenplay by Julius J Epstein, Philip G Epstein and Harold Koch, based on a play by M Burnett and J Alison

The Godfather Part II, screenplay by Francis Ford Coppola and Mario Puzo

As Good As It Gets, screenplay by James L Brooks and Mark Andrus

Chinatown, screenplay by Robert Towne

Jaws, screenplay by Peter Benchley and Carl Gottlieb

Juno, screenplay by Diablo Cody

In Bruges, screenplay *by* Martin McDonagh

In The Name Of The Father, adapted by Terry George and Jim Sheridan from the autobiography, *Proved Innocent: The Story of Gerry Conlon of the Guildford Four* by Gerry *Conlon*

Maudie, screenplay by Sherry White

Michael Collins, screenplay by Neil Jordan

Mulholland Drive, screenplay by David Lynch

One Flew Over the Cuckoo's Nest, screenplay by Laurence Hauben and Bo Goldman, based on novel by Ken Kesey.

On the Waterfront, screenplay by Budd Schulberg

Psycho, screenplay by Joseph Stefano

Slacker (1991), screenplay by Richard Linklater

Star Wars (1977), screenplay by George Lucas

Taxi Driver, screenplay by Paul Schrader

Terminator 2, screenplay by James Cameron and William Wisher

The Lady in the Van, screenplay by Alan Bennett

The Maltese Falcon, screenplay by John Huston, based on Dashiell Hammett's novel.

The Player, screenplay by Michael Tolkin

The Truman Show, screenplay by Andrew Niccol

Who's Afraid of Virginia Woolf?, screenplay by Ernest Lehman, based on the play of the same name by Edward Albee

Witness, screenplay by William Kelley, Pamela Wallace and Earl W Wallace

Acknowledgements

Huge thanks to all the people who have hired me as a screenwriter, but also to all those who have invited me to run courses and workshops on screenwriting since 1996. I've had the pleasure to teach screenwriting in universities, colleges and libraries, on panels and at festivals all over Ireland and farther afield in South Africa. Not to mention my regular slot with Filmbase in Dublin.

Thank you also to all the tutors I have had over the years, to the mentors, the speakers and the wonderful writers of inspiring books on screenwriting. To you all, I am immensely grateful. I'd especially like to mention Brian Dunnigan who ran the screenwriting course at the Northern Film School in Leeds Met. University when I attended in 1997-9.

Thank you also to all my students who have survived my classes and workshops!

Three factors allowed me to write this book now. One was Alan Fitzpatrick in Filmbase getting excited when I mentioned the idea. The second was my Maynooth University and Kildare County Council Library & Arts Service residency 2016-7. Without this, I'm not sure my head would have been clear enough to write this book, so thank you Maria Pramaggiore, Oona Frawley and Lucina Russeil.

The third impetus was realising I'd been teaching screenwriting for 21 years. I loved every minute and still do. It seemed time to try and distil it all down in one document.

A huge thank you to my editors, Lucille Redmond and Jean O'Sullivan and to my brave beta readers: Anita Murphy, Emma Quigley, Alan Fitzpatrick, Patrick O'Sullivan, Aaron Hunter, Nicolas Courdouan, Paul Farren and Steven Galvin. Your feedback was invaluable.

I am also immensely grateful to be surrounded by people who believe in me and my writing. To Caroline O'Farrell and Trish Groves and to my daughter Libby who has vowed never to become a writer (though I suspect she will), thank you. Also to Leo Lundy for still somehow thinking it's cool to live with a writer and to Javaholics cafe in Fairview where I escape to write, inspired by Al's flat whites.

I suspect there are more writers in there around me but we disguise ourselves well.

To Aisli Madden of DesignBOS (www.designbos.ie) for her wonderful cover.

To Barbara Henkes for the photo of me.

About the writer

Having worked as a journalist, L. J. Sedgwick moved into screenwriting in the 1990s, initially writing scripts for a number of series on RTE, the Irish national public service broadcaster and now has over eight hours of film and TV credits.

Her screenwriting credits span genres and form, from feature films, television drama and children's series to short films, radio plays and game narrative. *Punky*, her award-winning animation series, has been recognised as the first mainstream cartoon series in the world in which the main character has special needs. It is now available globally.

A graduate of the first Gregory Peck New York University Film School (1993), with an MA in Film and TV in Leeds (1999), she regularly teaches screenwriting and runs writing workshops throughout Ireland in libraries, colleges, universities and at festivals.

For more information, interviews and school or literary event queries, please contact Lindsay via books@lindsayjsedgwick.com or visit her website www.lindsayjsedgwick.com.

And if you have time, comments or reviews would be hugely appreciated on Amazon, Smashwords, Goodreads or on social media.

Contact details for Janey Mac Books: https://janeymacbooks.ecwid.com/.

Other books by this author

Dad's Red Dress

Jessie wants her family to be 'normal'. It's never going to happen. Kid sister, Laura (7) thinks she's been abducted by the Virgin Mary (twice; once on a motorbike). Step-mum Eva makes feminist installations, while Dad becomes Mandy as soon as the front door closes. Which is fine. Jessie loves them all to bits but they've just moved back to Ireland and this time she wants to try and avoid the bullying that usually kicks off when some school friend finds out about Dad.

Trouble is, she really has no control over what's about to happen.

"Filled with vivid, genuine characters and complex, conflicting family drama, it is joyous, loving and truly unique among the vast canon of coming-of-age stories... a delight to read. Simply wonderful." - Children's Books Ireland

"A beautiful story excellently told. One of the best novels I've read in bloody ages." - Patrick Chapman, author of *Slow Clocks of Decay*

"What a great story, filled with complexity - original and believable, every character so well developed... Jessie is just a delight, I was with her all the way! A beautiful relationship with her Dad, and her little sister! It's wonderful, just wonderful!!" - Caroline Farrell, author of *Arkyne* and *Lady Beth*.

The Angelica Touch

Angelica, 14, has reached three conclusions. Firstly, her mother Molly, who manages a rundown hotel on the wild Drisogue peninsula in Donegal, is desperately lonely. (She's not.) Secondly, it's entirely her fault that Molly is still single. (It might be.) Thirdly, since she can hardly have a boyfriend of her own if Number 2 is true, it's up to her to find her mother a man. (It really isn't.)

Given her natural gift for matchmaking, her solution is to develop a dating website for her mum. With the questions devised by Angelica and best friend, Grace, what could possibly go wrong?

"Another gift of joy from Sedgwick… This is a wonderful, imaginative tale that will leave you smiling." – Fallen Stars Stories blog.

"Off the wall and gorgeous. I love every word!" – Maria MacDermottroe, actress

All books can be purchased on Amazon and select bookstores but also directly from **Janey Mac Books** . at https://janeymacbooks.ecwid.com/

Made in the USA
Columbia, SC
13 April 2018